A FIREFLY POCKET GUIDE

ANCIENT

INFANTRY
SWORD

ROMAN
COIN

LEATHER
HORSE MASK

WALL MOSAIC

A FIREFLY POCKET GUIDE

ANCIENT ROME

Written by
SUSAN McKEEVER

FLOOR
MOSAIC

MERCHANT
SHIP

GLADIATOR'S
HELMET

FIREFLY BOOKS

A FIREFLY BOOK

Project editor	Linda White
Art editor	Sarah Ponder
Senior editor	Laura Buller
Senior art editor	Helen Senior
Production	Catherine Semark
	Louise Barratt
Editorial consultant	Simon James
Picture research	Christine Rista
US editor	Jill Hamilton
US consultant	Nancy Thompson

First American edition, 1995
2 4 6 8 10 9 7 5 3 1

Published in Canada by Firefly Books Ltd.
250 Sparks Avenue, Willowdale,
Ontario M2H 2S4

Canadian Cataloguing in Publication Data

McKeever, Susan
Ancient Rome

(Firefly pocket guides)
Includes index.
ISBN 1–895565–43–X
1. Rome – History. 2. Rome – Social life and customs.
I. Title. II. Series.
DG209.M35 1995   937   C94 932528–7

Color reproduction by Colourscan, Singapore
Printed and bound in Italy by L.E.G.O.

CONTENTS

HOW TO USE THIS BOOK

These pages show you how to use *Pocket Guide: Ancient
Rome*. The book is divided into a number of sections,
which cover different aspects of ancient Roman life. At
the back of the book is a useful reference section. Each
new section begins with a page that lists its contents.

ROMAN LIFE
Ancient Rome has been divided
into subject areas and arranged
in eight sections, beginning
with "Introduction to ancient
Rome," which sets the scene
by providing an overview of
the subject and a brief history.

*Corner
coding*

Heading

Introduction

GAMES AND LEISURE

THE THEATER
THE ROMANS adopted the idea
of theater from the Greeks. A
first, translations of Greek plays
were performed. Later, original
plays were written by Roman
playwrights such as Plautus
and Terence. Comedies were preferred to
tragedies. Mime was a Roman invention,
but, unlike today's mime, actors spoke!

THEATER RUINS
The Romans built theaters all
over the empire, like this theater
of Aspendus in Asia Minor.

IN THE WINGS
In this mosaic a group of actors are preparing for a play.
Two actors are practicing dance steps, one actor is being
helped into his costume, and a musician is playing double
pipes. Masks lie ready to be worn at the performance.

*Poorer people
sat higher up.*

*Underneath the seats, a
network of corridors and
stairs allowed easy exit.*

112

Caption

CORNER CODING
Corners of the main
section pages are
color coded to
remind you which
section you are in.

■ INTRODUCTION TO
ANCIENT ROME

■ ROMAN SOCIETY

■ LIFE IN ROME

■ THE ROMAN ARMY

■ BUILDING AND
TECHNOLOGY

■ GAMES AND LEISURE

■ RELIGION, FESTIVALS,
AND DEATH

■ THE END OF AN ERA

HEADING
This describes the
subject of the page.
This page is about
the theater. If a
subject continues
over several pages,
then the same
heading applies.

INTRODUCTION
This provides a clear,
general overview of the
subject. After reading
the introduction, you
should have a good idea
what the pages are about.

CAPTIONS AND
ANNOTATIONS
Each illustration has a
caption. Annotations, in
italics, point out features
of an illustration and
usually have leader lines.

RUNNING HEADS

These remind you which section you are in. The top of the left-hand page gives the section name. The right-hand page gives the subject. Here, The Theater is in the Games and Leisure section.

FEATURE BOXES

Throughout the book, feature boxes supply extra information about aspects of Roman life, such as types of gladiator. The feature box on this page gives details about Roman theater masks.

FACT BOXES

The introductory pages to each of the eight sections have fact boxes. These contain interesting facts about the subject covered in that section.

Running head   *Feature box*

Annotation

LABELS

To give extra clarity, some pictures have labels. They may give extra information, or identify a picture when it is not obvious from the text what the picture actually is.

REFERENCE SECTION

The reference section pages are yellow and appear at the back of the book. On these, you will find useful facts, dates, and charts. This section includes a map showing the expansion of the Roman empire, a list of the Roman emperors, and a feature on Roman architecture.

GLOSSARY AND INDEX

There is a glossary and an index at the back of the book. The glossary defines and explains words and terms in this book that are specific to ancient Roman life. The index lists every subject alphabetically.

RIBVN

FELICI

ISQVE

QVE·

M·DOM

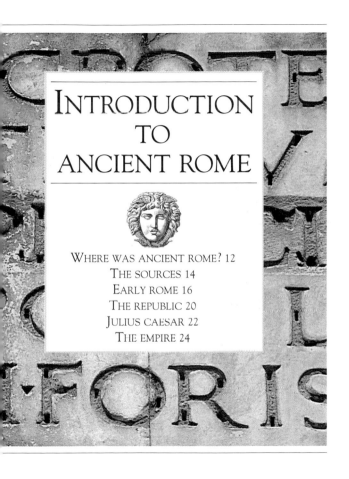

Introduction to Ancient Rome

WHERE WAS ANCIENT ROME?

THE CIVILIZATION WE KNOW as ancient Rome began nearly three thousand years ago in Rome, now the capital city of Italy. Although Rome gave its name to the civilization, the city was only a small part of the Roman empire, which grew over the centuries to become one of the largest the world has ever known. But the city of Rome remained its center, and all roads in the empire eventually led there.

ROMA COIN
The goddess Roma was worshiped as the personification of the city of Rome.

FACTS ABOUT ROME

• The history of Rome can be divided into three periods: the rule of kings (c.753-509 B.C.), the Republic (c.509-31 B.C.), and the Empire, when the Roman empire was ruled by emperors (c.31 B.C.-A.D. 476).

• Senators served in the Senate for life.

• In 46 B.C. Julius Caesar established the calendar still basically used today. To do this he added an extra 67 days to 45 B.C.

THE CITY OF ROME TODAY
Today, millions of tourists flock to Rome to visit its many attractions. Thanks to the building skills of the Romans, people can still see temples, statues, monuments, and arches that were built in the days of the empire.

Tiber River

Ponte Sant'Angelo

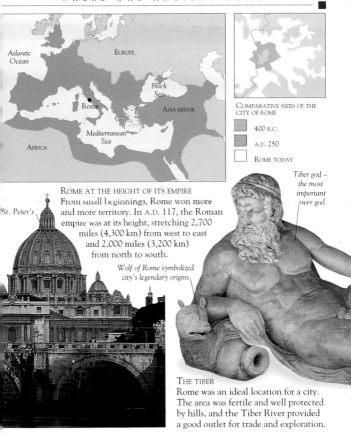

COMPARATIVE SIZES OF THE CITY OF ROME

400 B.C.

A.D. 250

ROME TODAY

ROME AT THE HEIGHT OF ITS EMPIRE
From small beginnings, Rome won more and more territory. In A.D. 117, the Roman empire was at its height, stretching 2,700 miles (4,300 km) from west to east and 2,000 miles (3,200 km) from north to south.

Wolf of Rome symbolized city's legendary origins

Tiber god – the most important river god

THE TIBER
Rome was an ideal location for a city. The area was fertile and well protected by hills, and the Tiber River provided a good outlet for trade and exploration.

THE SOURCES

OUR KNOWLEDGE of ancient Rome comes from the variety of artifacts that remain from Roman times. The Romans left behind buildings, art, and everyday items. Writings by people of the time have also survived – these tell about daily life, politics, and history. Monks in medieval times transcribed the original writings.

MOSAIC
Artists' work, such as this mosaic depicting a Roman birdbath, provides valuable information about the times in which the artist lived.

HORSE MASK
Objects ranging from pots and pans to jewelry and shoes have been found on Roman sites. This is a replica of a leather mask found in Britain.

RECONSTRUCTION
With only scant remains, archaeologists can create a remarkably clear picture of people from the past. From a skull, archaeologists are able to build up the musculature over the existing bone structure, until a facial shape of the deceased person emerges.

Bone is cleaned   Skull is "clothed"   A face emerges

THE SKULL   MUSCLE AND NERVES   AN ANCIENT ROMAN

Marcus Agrippa built the original Pantheon.

M·AGRIPPA·L·F·COS·TERTIVM·FECIT

STONE INSCRIPTIONS
The Romans made inscriptions on many of their buildings. The information is accessible because these inscriptions were written in Latin.

THE BUILDINGS OF ANCIENT ROME
Many Roman buildings have survived almost unchanged. They reveal architectural styles, building materials, and town planning. The location of the buildings also shows the extent of the empire. These ruins are from a huge *villa* that emperor Hadrian built near Rome.

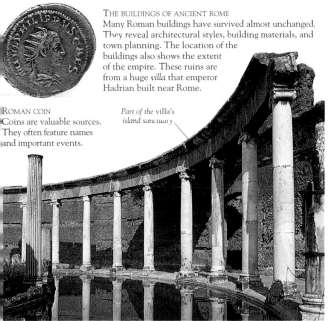

ROMAN COIN
Coins are valuable sources. They often feature names and important events.

Part of the villa's island sanctuary

EARLY ROME

BEFORE ROME'S RISE to power, the land of Italy was occupied by a variety of settlers. Among them were Greeks, Etruscans, Samnites, Latins, Sabines, and Umbrians. The Latins, who lived on the Latium plains by the Tiber River, were natives of early Rome. Over a period of time, they conquered all the other peoples who were sharing Italy with them.

ETRUSCAN WARRIOR

Etruscans and Greeks

A long time before Romulus's legendary founding of Rome, the Etruscans lived in Etruria, north of the city. They also had settlements in the south. The Etruscans had a thriving civilization based on trade and agriculture. The Greeks colonized areas in southern Italy and Sicily, where they built many fine houses and temples. Both the Greeks and Etruscans had a huge effect on early Rome in terms of art, architecture, religion, and technology.

ETRUSCAN VOTIVE OFFERING

GREEK	OTTO-UMBRIAN
LATIN	ETRUSCAN

MAP OF PRE-ROMAN ITALY
Pre-Roman Italy was a land of many different cultures and languages. The Sabines, living to the north of Rome, and the Samnites, who lived in central Italy, were both part of the Otto-Umbrian tribes. All these peoples influenced Roman culture as Rome began to expand.

16

SARCOPHAGUS FOR HUSBAND AND WIFE
Etruscans believed in life after death.
The dead were buried with jewelry,
artifacts, and food for the next life.
Wealthy people could afford to have
elaborate underground tombs. This
5th-century B.C. sarcophagus shows
a dead couple feasting at a banquet.

Terracotta coffin

*This intricate painting
depicts figures from
Greek mythology.*

GRECIAN URN
The Greeks were
skilled artists.
They produced
exquisite pottery,
metalwork, and
sculptures. Greek
pottery was very
popular in Rome.

Samnite gladiator

Long shield

SAMNITE WARRIOR
The Romans copied their
long rectangular shields
from Samnite warriors.
One type of gladiator
dressed as a Samnite.

*This urn is
from the 4th
century B.C.*

Facts and fiction

Legend claims that Rome was
founded in 753 B.C. by twins
called Romulus and Remus.
Although no one knows if this
story is true, it is certain that
the site of the future city was
being settled by farmers at
about this time. This small
community on the seven hills
surrounding the Tiber River
grew over time into the city
of Rome. For more than 200
years, the city was ruled by
kings. The monarchy was later
ousted in favor of a republic.

MARS, GOD OF WAR
Legend says that
Mars, the god
of war, was the
father of Romulus
and Remus. Their
mother was King
Numitor's daughter.

THE SEVEN HILLS OF ROME
Tribes of Latins lived on the seven hills
of Rome, making a living by farming.
They defended their hilltop settlements
from other tribes that lived nearby.
The marshy valley in the middle was
later to become the site of the forum.

AENEAS THE TROJAN WARRIOR
After his city was destroyed by the Greeks,
Aeneas founded a new "Troy" in Italy.
Many years later, King Numitor, Aeneas's
descendant, was driven out of his city by
his wicked brother, Amulius. When
Numitor's daughter gave birth to twin
sons, Amulius feared a threat to his power

ROMULUS AND REMUS

Wicked Amulius ordered that the twins be drowned in the Tiber. Luckily, the boys were saved. They grew up to found a new city at the place where they were rescued. But Romulus killed Remus during a petty quarrel and became Rome's first king.

Legend tells that a she-wolf suckled the twins.

FRIEZE SHOWING LEGEND OF AENEAS

Thatched roof

Wattle and daub walls

IRON-AGE HUT

The earliest settlers in Rome lived in simple huts. We know this from evidence such as post holes left in the soil and small models of huts found in ancient graves.

Tarquinius Superbus (Tarquin the Proud) is said to have been a cruel king

RENAISSANCE PAINTING DEPICTING FOUNDING OF TEMPLE OF JUPITER

THE LAST KING

Following the reign of Romulus, Latin, Sabine, and finally a line of Etruscan kings ruled Rome until 509 B.C. The last king of Rome, Tarquin the Proud, was a tyrant, so the people drove him out and set up a republic.

THE REPUBLIC

IN THE ROMAN REPUBLIC, the power lay not with one person but with a group of people called senators, who met together in the Senate. Every year, Roman citizens voted to select certain senators to be government officials. All senators came from wealthy Roman families. Since the majority of citizens were poor, they often felt badly represented by the government.

THE SENATE HOUSE
This building in Rome is a reconstruction of the Senate house, where a council of powerful men met to make decisions about government policy.

Atlas was one of many gods worshiped by Romans.

RELIGIOUS OFFICIALS
These men supervised public worship of the state gods and looked after sacrifices and festivals. Top official was the *pontifex maximus*, a position later held by the emperor.

STRUCTURE OF THE ROMAN REPUBLIC
Elected from the Senate were *consuls*, *quaestors*, *aediles*, *praetors*, and religious officials. There were also *censors*, who revised Senate membership and issued contracts for temples and roads. The initials *SPQR*, meaning "the Senate and people of Rome," were put on buildings, army standards, and coins.

Chariot race

Pompey held the office of consul twice.

AEDILES

Four *aediles* held office to look after public buildings, sewers, streets, and traffic and to provide markets. *Aediles* were also responsible for putting on the public games, and so they often became very popular with the people.

PRAETORS

Second in power to the *consuls*, eight *praetors* were elected to manage Rome's legal system. When provinces abroad were added, provincial governors also acted as *praetors*.

BUST OF POMPEY

Ax and rods symbolized a praetor's *authority to punish*.

QUAESTORS AND PROCURATORS

These officials were in charge of Rome's finances. As Rome grew in size, they increased in number. This was the official brand of the *procurator* of Britain. He used it to collect taxes and pay the army.

CONSULS

Every year, two *consuls* were elected. These men were the most senior officials in the government and were advised by the Senate. To avoid tyranny, each *consul* had the power to veto the other. So, both had to agree on a decision. In times of trouble, the Senate could elect a *dictator*, who had absolute power.

JULIUS CAESAR

IN REPUBLICAN ROME, a number of generals became very powerful. One of these was Julius Caesar. After serving in a number of government positions, he was elected *consul* in 59 B.C. Caesar's army won large territories for Rome, but his power worried the Senate, and they ordered him to give up his army. He refused, marched on Rome, and seized power as dictator.

CAESAR, THE FIRST LIVING
ROMAN TO APPEAR ON A COIN

This relief of Cleopatra is from the temple of Hathor in Egypt.

DATELINE

100 B.C. Born in Rome.

59 B.C. Elected *consul*.

58 B.C. Begins successful Gaul campaign.

55 B.C. Invades Britain.

49 B.C. Marches on Rome and seizes power.

48 B.C. Defeats Pompey.

44 B.C. Declared dictator for life.

44 B.C. Murdered by a group of senators.

CLEOPATRA

Caesar's defiance of the Senate led to civil war. He fought battles all over the empire. During his time in Egypt, Caesar and Queen Cleopatra became lovers and she bore him a son.

CAESAR'S CONQUESTS
Africa Nova in North Africa was added to the
empire by Caesar, but his most significant conquest
was Gaul (France, Switzerland, Belgium, and part
of Germany). This painting shows the proud Gallic
leader, Vercingetorix, about to surrender to Caesar.

INVASION OF BRITAIN
Not all of Caesar's
campaigns were
successful. His
attempts
to invade Britain
were thwarted
by the Britons'
fierce resistance.

*British warriors wore twisted
necklaces called torcs.*

BUST OF CAESAR
Julius Caesar had an aristocratic
upbringing. He was a great orator
and became very popular with
the common people.

DEATH OF CAESAR
This coin commemorates
the murder of Julius Caesar.
It gives the date, the "ides"
(or 15th) of March, and shows
two daggers, the murder weapons.

THE EMPIRE

AFTER CAESAR'S DEATH, civil wars raged until only two men remained in the struggle for power: former *consul* Mark Antony and Caesar's adopted son Octavian. Antony ruled in the East, and Octavian ruled the West. But conflict between the two led to war. After a huge sea battle at Actium in 31 B.C., Octavian emerged as Rome's sole ruler.

LAUREL LEAVES
Emperors wore wreaths of laurel leaves instead of crowns. Laurel crowns had originally been worn by generals to celebrate their military victories.

The first emperor

Octavian was renamed Augustus, meaning "majestic." After the turmoil of civil war, the Roman people were desperate for a strong ruler. Augustus was very careful to keep the idea of the Republic alive and said he was simply "first citizen," one of the people. But he was in fact the first emperor – the Republic was dead and the period of Rome's history known as the Empire had begun.

DATELINE

63 B.C. Born in Rome.

31 B.C. Defeats Mark Antony at Actium.

29 B.C. Declares peace throughout the Roman world.

27 B.C. Given the name "Augustus."

A.D. 14 Dies. Senate declares him a god.

BUST OF AUGUSTUS
A patron of the arts, Augustus was thought to be very handsome.

Altar

Frieze shows members of the emperor's family

LIVIA
Livia was the wife of Augustus for 53 years and exerted great influence over him.

COIN
This is one of the coins Antony struck to pay his troops during the power struggle with Augustus.

Roman warship

PEACE
Following all the civil wars, Augustus declared peace throughout the Roman world. This monument was built to celebrate the Augustan peace.

BUILDING WORK
Augustus boasted, "I found Rome built of bricks. I leave her covered in marble." He carried out much restoration work on existing buildings and erected a new forum.

Ruins of Augustus's forum in Rome

The emperors

Rome continued to be ruled by emperors for centuries after the death of Augustus. However, they did not all rule wisely. Some seem to have been mad; others were corrupt. At first, there were dynasties whereby emperors were succeeded by members of their family. Later, the army influenced who came to power, and successful generals were often declared emperor by their troops. By the 2nd century A.D., there were emperors from the provinces.

MUREX SHELL

NERO (RULED A.D. 54-68)
Nero was only 16 when he came to power. At first he did what the Senate asked. Later, he became tyrannical. He had his stepbrother, mother, and wife murdered. It is said that he set fire to Rome to build his palace.

Nero erected a colossal statue of himself in Rome.

PURPLE DYE
Purple was the color usually worn by emperors (for anyone else to dress entirely in purple was treason). The dye was distilled from murex seashells.

Tiberius

Portrait of emperor

CALIGULA (A.D. 37-41)

Said to be insane, Caligula took his horse into the Senate and tried to have it elected as *consul*. He was cruel and unpredictable. The Praetorian Guard finally murdered him.

An illness left Caligula deranged.

TRAJAN (A.D. 98-117)

This arch was built in honor of Trajan, an emperor born in Spain. When he conquered Dacia, the empire reached its largest. In Rome, he built Trajan's markets, a huge complex of shops and offices.

MARCUS AURELIUS (A.D. 161-180)

This benevolent ruler encouraged rich citizens to donate money to the poor. This column commemorates his successful defense of the empire against the barbarian invaders.

Legion's standard

TIBERIUS (A.D. 14-37)

This scabbard has pictures of Tiberius. He ruled well at first, but he became terrified of plots to kill him and forced many people to commit suicide.

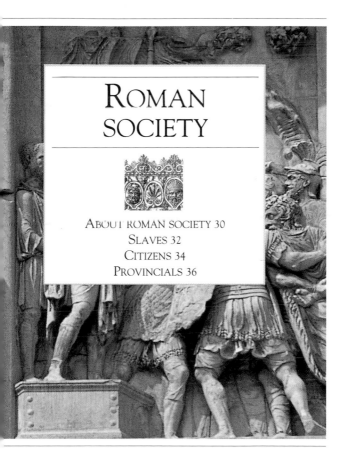

ROMAN
SOCIETY

ABOUT ROMAN SOCIETY

THE PEOPLE OF ROME fell neatly into two groups: citizens and noncitizens. To be born a citizen brought many advantages, because a noncitizen was denied certain rights. Roman citizens were divided into three classes, according to wealth. Noncitizens were either provincials or slaves. A woman's position in Roman society depended on the status of her husband.

ROMAN FAMILIES
The *paterfamilias*, or father, was all-powerful. He was in charge of his wife and children, the slaves, and all the possessions in the house.

Tunic and cloak

ROMAN CITIZEN
(2ND-CENTURY-A.D. STATUE)

BECOMING A CITIZEN
A boy had a "growing up" ceremony at the age of 14. He gave up his *bulla* (a charm worn around the neck) and became a registered citizen.

PROVINCIALS
The Romans conquered many lands outside Italy. People living in these lands were provincials. This plaque comes from a province in North Africa.

WOMEN IN SOCIETY

Roman women were not educated to a high standard and they could not vote or hold any government position. Married women spent their time engaged in household tasks; the wealthy had slaves to help them. Widows were able to control their own property.

SOCIETY FACTS

• Most craftworkers and artists were slaves.

• Children of freed slaves became citizens.

• Intermarriage with provincials extended citizen's rights to them.

• A *paterfamilias* had the power to condemn his family to death.

The groom holds a written contract of marriage.

Clasped hands symbolize union of couple and their families

GETTING MARRIED

Most marriages were arranged for financial or political reasons. The wedding usually took place at the bride's house and was witnessed by family and friends. The bride wore a special dress and a bright orange veil.

SLAVES

THE LOWEST RANK in Roman society was that of slave. Slaves had no legal rights; they were owned by Romans who put them to work in their homes and fields. People became slaves when the Romans conquered their lands and took them prisoner. Any children they had were then born into slavery. Many slaves were treated very badly, but others were granted their freedom. Educated Greek slaves were highly prized and often worked as doctors and tutors.

EDUCATED SLAVES
Many slaves were well educated and artistic. Musicians, dancers, actors, and teachers were usually slaves.

Prisoners of war

SPOILS OF WAR
Prisoners captured in wars were taken to slave markets and auctioned off to the public. A slave became the property of the highest bidder. This detail from Trajan's Column shows a group of captured Dacians destined for the slave market.

FREEDMEN
Slaves could be freed by their masters or save up to buy their freedom. Known as freedmen, they were not full citizens, but they had more rights than slaves and often owned businesses. This relief marks the tomb of a group of freedmen.

FIGHTING FOR FREEDOM
Gladiators, who were usually slaves, had the chance to win their freedom by success in the arena. A wooden sword was presented to the gladiator to signify his freedom.

Gladiator's shield

Slave styles mistress's hair

ATTENDING THE RICH
Wealthy households had several slaves responsible for various tasks such as cleaning and cooking. This picture shows the mistress of the house having her hair done by two slaves.

CITIZENS

ROMAN CITIZENS had certain rights and duties that did not apply to noncitizens. Citizens could vote in the yearly elections, work in government, and be entertained at the public games – but they also had to pay taxes. Citizenship was restricted to people born of free (nonslave) parents, at first in Rome, but later throughout Italy. In A.D. 212 an edict extended these rights to the entire Roman empire.

Shoulder plate

Flexible metal strips

Only legionaries were issued with this highly protective armor.

Woolen tunic

GRAIN DOLE
Citizens of Rome were entitled to an allowance of free grain, which was made into bread and distributed as loaves. By A.D. 14 some 300,000 people were on the dole.

JOINING THE ARMY
Only citizens could have a decent career in the army. Noncitizens could not be legionaries, the backbone of the army, but they could be auxiliaries. Provincials who joined these support forces were rewarded with citizenship at the end of service.

RANKS OF CITIZENS

The three orders of citizens were senators, equestrians (descendants of the first cavalry officers), and the people. All citizens wore togas on formal occasions; a senator's toga had wide purple borders.

GAMES

All citizens could go to the games. The expression "bread and circuses" describes the free bread and lavish games the government put on to keep the people happy.

This emperor was a powerful military leader.

FIRST CITIZEN

When Augustus became the first emperor, he knew people would be worried that Rome was returning to the rule of kings, so he called himself *princeps*, or "first citizen." After him, all emperors were regarded as first citizens.

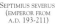

SEPTIMIUS SEVERUS
(EMPEROR FROM
A.D. 193-211)

PROVINCIALS

THE MAJOR PART of the vast Roman empire was the provinces. These were lands that the Romans had conquered. Although some subject peoples were already citizens – often by completing service in the Roman army – in A.D. 212 the emperor Caracalla extended citizenship to all provincials. This enabled him to tax more people.

GOVERNOR'S CHAIR
To look after the various provinces, the emperor appointed governors. They sat on special chairs, like the one shown here.

Spain and North Africa

Spain quickly became Romanized after its occupation. Its oldest town, Italica, produced two emperors: Trajan and Hadrian. Spain had mines supplying precious metals. It also exported olive oil, wine, and fish sauce. Africa was first occupied in 146 B.C. after the wars with Carthage. It was a rich province, supplying many types of wild animals for the arena, as well as purple dye, olive oil, and grain.

PROVINCES OF THE ROMAN EMPIRE
This map depicts the Roman empire at its greatest extent. The darker area shows the Roman provinces of Spain and North Africa.

SPAIN

NORTH AFRICA

| EMPIRE AT ITS HEIGHT | SPAIN AND NORTH AFRICA |

SILVER GOBLET
Spain's precious metals were used to make vessels like this goblet as well as exquisite jewelry.

Many thousands of wild animals perished in Rome's arenas.

WILD ANIMAL TRADE
The town of Leptis Magna in Africa specialized in the trade of wild animals and became very wealthy, spending lavishly to erect magnificent buildings.

Musical instruments

MOSAIC OF A LEOPARD

PROVINCIAL-STYLE VILLA
The provinces retained their own architectural styles, but there were also buildings just like those in Rome. Some buildings were a mixture of Roman and provincial styles. The fortifications on this North African *villa* were for defense against attack.

Lookout tower

Upper story

Enclosed first floor

Gaul, Britain, Greece, and Danube lands

Gaul and Germany were home to the Celts. The south was more urban, while the north and west were mainly agricultural. Fine crafts and jewelry were made here. Britain, a rich province, provided many goods. Greece was a thriving civilization that greatly influenced Rome. The Danube provinces had many military forts and supplied soldiers for the army.

MARBLE
Rome used marble from Greece in many of its finest buildings.

PORTA NIGRA
Augustus created a flourishing city at Trier, northeast Gaul (now Germany). The Porta Nigra ("black gate") was later added to protect against barbarian invasions.

EMPIRE AT ITS HEIGHT

GAUL, BRITAIN, GREECE, DANUBE

PROVINCIAL MAP
When Dacia (modern Romania) fell to Rome in A.D. 106, the Roman empire was at its biggest.

DOG BROOCH
Exports from Gaul included pottery, hunting dogs, and intricate jewelry such as this bronze brooch.

DACIA
Trajan's Column was built to commemorate the emperor's conquest of Dacia. This detail shows a river god watching Roman troops cross the Danube.

Tiers of arched windows

Face skillfully wrought from iron

IRON MASK
Britain had a large army presence. In peacetime, soldiers would take part in cavalry sports for fun. They wore masks such as this one and fought mock battles on horseback.

VIENNE (FRANCE)
During Roman times, this Gaulish city grew rich due to its surrounding agricultural land. Public buildings, such as this fine temple, can still be seen today.

Egypt and the East

Alexandria, the capital of Egypt and an important cultural center, was the second largest city in the Roman empire. Most of the grain that fed the empire came from Egypt and was shipped from Alexandria. The province also supplied papyrus for writing, flax, olives, and dates. The eastern provinces exported exotic goods such as silks, spices, dyes, and perfumes. Camel trains carried goods from as far away as India and China to one of the coastal ports for export.

PALMYRA
Trade links with the East made this Syrian city very prosperous.

SWEET-SMELLING THINGS
Perfumes, spices, and flowers came to Rome from the East. This painting shows a woman pouring perfume into a vial.

Alexandria

EGYPT

☐ EMPIRE AT ITS HEIGHT   ■ EGYPT AND THE EAST

PROVINCIAL MAP
Egypt became Roman in 30 B.C. The eastern provinces had all been added by the early 2nd century A.D.

SCENE FROM THE RIVER NILE

Alexandria was a center of art in the 1st century B.C., producing many frescoes and mosaics. Egyptian scenes became very fashionable. This Pompeii mosaic depicts Nile wildlife.

EMPEROR

This coin shows Philip the Arab, another Roman emperor who came from one of the provinces. He was born in Syria and reigned from A.D. 244-49.

Family members are wearing a range of exotic headgear.

Tunic and pants

EASTERN FAMILY

Roman provinces often kept much of their original culture. This tomb mosaic from Syria shows an upper class family group. They are wearing eastern-style clothing and they would have spoken either in Greek or Syriac.

Eastern slippers rather than Roman sandals

4 1

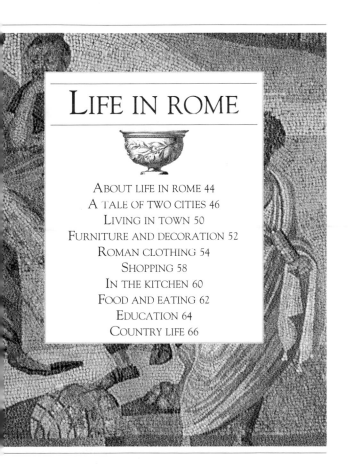

LIFE IN ROME

ABOUT LIFE IN ROME

THE LIFE-STYLE of an ancient Roman depended very much on income. The wealthy owned splendid houses with ornate decorations and had a staff of slaves to attend to every whim. These fortunate Romans wore fine clothes and ate sumptuous fare. At the other end of the scale, poor people lived in squalid accommodations and could afford only simple and basic food.

JEWELRY
Wealthy Romans wore jewelry made from gold and precious gems. Poorer people settled for more modest items made from bronze or glass.

STREET SCENE
The streets of Roman towns were lively and crowded places, lined with every type of shop. Town dwellers squeezed along the narrow sidewalks, rubbing shoulders with street vendors and musicians.

Reconstructed wooden balcony

Mud from the eruption of Vesuvius in A.D. 79 kept this Herculaneum building intact.

FEMALE SCHOLAR

EDUCATION
Women in Rome seldom got more than a basic education. Higher studies were strictly for the men, who were groomed for careers in the government. Poorer Romans, male or female, rarely received any education at all.

DECORATIONS

Houses often looked drab from the outside because the Romans were more interested in interior decoration. Inside, walls and floors were covered with paintings and mosaics. Elegant statues of gods, animals, or people stood in rooms and gardens.

COUNTRY PURSUITS

Many Romans lived in the countryside. The poor farmed land rented from rich landowners and sold excess produce. The wealthy retreated to the countryside for vacations and engaged in pursuits such as hunting, seen in this relief.

Boy removing thorn from foot

LAMPLIGHT

Oil-burning lamps, made from pottery or bronze, provided the Romans with light. A large lamp might have 14 wicks.

Hole for wick

BRONZE SCULPTURE

LIVING IN ROME FACTS

• One million people lived in the city of Rome by A.D. 1.

• Romans washed their dishes by rubbing them with sand, then rinsing.

• Lead poisoning was common because of lead cooking utensils.

A TALE OF TWO CITIES

A GREAT TRAGEDY within the Roman empire left a treasure trove of priceless information. On August 24, A.D. 79, near Naples in Italy, the long-dormant volcano Vesuvius erupted, burying towns around it in burning ash, stone, and pumice. After three days the sky cleared, but the two worst hit towns, Pompeii and Herculaneum, were virtually forgotten for many centuries.

PLINY THE YOUNGER
This scholar saw the eruption from across the Bay of Naples and recorded it in writing.

MOUNT VESUVIUS ERUPTS
Everyone thought that Vesuvius was extinct. The mountain had not erupted for 800 years, and its tranquil slopes were covered in vineyards, farmhouses, and *villas*. During the eruption, ash and pumice blasted from the summit, landing up to 12 miles (20 km) away.

MAP OF DESTRUCTION
Right after the eruption, burning ash and pumice rained down on Pompeii. Only a little ash blew in Herculaneum's direction. But the next morning, surges of hot ash and gas and waves of boiling mud engulfed the entire town.

POMPEII SCENE
Today, the ruined streets of Pompeii still lie in the shadow of Vesuvius. On the day of the eruption, many of the town's 20,000 inhabitants escaped, running through the rain of ash. The next day, the 2,000 people who stayed all perished.

HERCULANEUM – OLD AND NEW
The new town of Herculaneum stands above the deeply buried Roman ruins. Vesuvius looms in the background.

DEPTH OF ASH
The town of Pompeii was buried under 13 ft (4 m) of volcanic debris. Herculaneum was buried beneath 66 ft (20 m) of debris, the result of six surges of hot ash and gas and six mud flows.

66 FT (20 M)

49 FT (15 M)

33 FT (10 M)

16 FT (5 M)

13 FT (4 M)

10 FT (3 M)

7 FT (2 M)

3 FT (1 M)

Flow of hot ash, pumice, and rock

Surge of hot gas and ash

First, a rain of ash and stones buried Pompeii.

Cities preserved

The abrupt burial of two towns allowed us to learn minute details about people's lives. Excavations began in the 18th century, and slowly a picture of everyday life in both towns emerged. Pompeii was a thriving trading center; Herculaneum was a fashionable seaside resort. Shops and bakeries lined the paved streets, and there were grand public buildings, such as theaters, temples, and bathhouses.

LOAF OF BREAD

PRESERVED EGGS

FOOD
Hot ash and gas turned the food to carbon. This loaf of bread, similar to modern Italian bread, was found in the oven of a Pompeii bakery.

Wet volcanic mud preserved bones but not body shape.

DOG MOSAIC
Many paintings and artifacts were preserved by the tragedy. This floor mosaic comes from a Pompeii entryway. The dog was there to warn off trespassers.

HERCULANEUM SKELETON
In 1982, hundreds of skeletons were found in boat chambers in Herculaneum's ancient seawall. Before this, only a few bodies had been found in the town, and it had been believed that nearly everyone had escaped.

PLASTER CAST PROCESS
Ash and pumice set around the Pompeiians' bodies. When the bodies decayed, hollow shapes remained in hard rock. Wet plaster was poured into the hollows.

The body cavity is discovered, filled with bones.

Plaster is poured into the cavity through a small hole.

MOTHER AND CHILD
Here, a mother and child lie side by side, the mother trying to protect her offspring from the poisonous fumes.

Plaster cast preserves details

Casts show the Pompeiians in their death throes.

Victim tries to shield face

BABY
This suffocated baby was found in the area now called the Garden of the Fugitives.

MAN
This man was discovered crouching against the wall of the athletics stadium. He is trying to hide his face from the fumes. Most of those who died were suffocated.

LIVING IN TOWN

ROMAN TOWNS were bustling, noisy places. Only the privileged few could afford to live in a town house, or *domus*, a peaceful, private retreat that had no windows in the wall facing the road. By contrast, most people lived in apartment buildings, called *insulae*, with windows opening onto the streets and all their chaos.

Clay tiles, made from a mold

People ate while reclining on couches in the dining room, or triclinium.

Cheap rooms had no running water.

Walls facing the street were windowless.

The more affluent occupants lived in well-furnished, comfortable rooms.

The shops at the bottom created a lot of noise.

Balcony

Streets were dirty.

A HOME IN AN APARTMENT BUILDING
A typical *insula* might have three or four stories. The higher people lived, the worse the conditions were. On the first floor there were shops. Second-floor apartments had several rooms. At the top, rooms were small and cramped.

BEAUTIFUL TOWN HOUSE

Most Roman town houses followed the same plan. The *atrium*, or entrance hall, had a central opening in the roof to let in light. There was also an *impluvium*, a pool to catch rainwater. Various rooms led off the *atrium*. At the back was often a colonnaded garden, called a *peristyle*.

Colonnaded garden

Many slaves were employed as maids, cooks, porters, and companions.

Bedroom

The family worshiped daily at the lararium, a shrine to the household gods.

Flushing toilets were connected to the town's sewers.

Impluvium

Mosaic floor

Guests were received in the atrium.

INSULAE AT OSTIA, NEAR ROME

These surviving *insulae* are solidly built of stone. *Insulae* were often made of flimsy wood and soared five stories high. Overcrowding and ramshackle extensions caused frequent fires, and often whole buildings collapsed.

FURNITURE AND DECORATION

THE ROMANS had surprisingly little furniture in their homes. The lack of clutter made rooms appear elegant and airy, allowing full appreciation of exquisite statues and the fine paintings and mosaics that adorned floors, walls, and ceilings. A *domus* or *villa* might have beds, couches, cupboards, tables, chairs, stools, and oil lamps. The rich spent a lot of money on marble, bronze, and rare inlaid woods.

DECORATIVE MOLDING
Intricate stucco reliefs, which blended with paintings and mosaics to form decorative panels, were a feature of many private houses.

Cupids harvesting grapes

WALL PAINTING
The walls of luxury houses were painted with scenes that reflected every aspect of Roman life. This painting shows a group of women talking.

CAMEO VASE
This vase would have taken great skill to make. White glass was cut away over blue glass to make the pattern.

WALL MOSAIC DEPICTING NEPTUNE AND SALACIA

Mosaics covered many floors and walls. Skilled artisans worked from drawn plans, pressing tiny pieces of colored glass or stone into wet plaster to make a picture or design. The subjects ranged from rural life to gods and goddesses.

TABLE LEG
Legs of tables were often ornamented with clawed or hoofed feet. This leg is from a three-legged marble table.

Inlaid couch end

Stool

COUCH
One of the most important pieces of furniture was the couch. This was used for sleeping, eating, or simply reclining. Sometimes couches were high and had to be reached by a little stool. At dinner parties, a couch would accommodate three people lying side by side.

ROMAN CLOTHING

ROMAN FABRICS decayed long ago, but we know about the clothes people wore from paintings, statues, and carvings. Most clothing was made from wool or linen – luxury fabrics such as cotton or silk were expensive and had to be imported from India and China. The most common item of clothing was a loose-fitting tunic, tied at the waist with a belt.

THE TOGA

Only citizens could wear the toga, a large piece of cloth wrapped around the body and flung over the shoulder. Togas were usually white. A senator wore a toga with a purple stripe.

Cloak

Children dressed much like their parents.

Pants

Bulla

Boots

Sandals

VARIOUS CLOTHING

Most poorer people wore just a tunic. In colder parts of the empire people wore woolen or felt cloaks, pants, and warm leather boots. Boys wore *bullas* (childhood charms) around their necks

Women often wore hairpieces.

Veils were a symbol of piety and protected hair from sun.

Palla

Stola

Sandals kept feet cool in warm climates.

CLOTHES FOR WOMEN

Over the tunic, married women wore a long, ankle-length tunic called a *stola*. They might then drape a shawl-like item called a *palla* over both. Wealthy women could afford to have their clothes made from brightly patterned silks and cottons.

ROMAN SANDALS

In hotter parts of the empire, footwear consisted mainly of leather sandals, well ventilated to keep feet cool. Designs were similar to today's sandals. Military sandals had tough hobnails on the soles.

FASTENING CLOTHES

Brooches, called *fibulae*, were often used to fasten clothing at the shoulder. They worked like safety pins and could be elaborately decorated.

Jewelry and adornment

Roman men and women took care of their appearance. Men visited the barber for hair and beard trims; fashionable women, attended by slaves, performed a lengthy morning toilet of hairdressing and makeup. Men wore rings and fastened their cloaks with decorative brooches called *fibulae*; women draped themselves in necklaces, tiaras, bracelets, anklets, and earrings, fashioned from gold, silver, and bronze, often set with precious stones.

DOLPHIN EARRINGS
Roman earrings looked much like those people wear today. These gold earrings were made for pierced ears.

Mirror

Lock

VANITY CASE
Women kept jewelry and other valuables in special boxes. The box above also contains a mirror, cosmetic tools, and hair accessories.

ADORNED WOMAN
This Pompeii mosaic shows how a well-to-do lady might have adorned herself. Her carefully styled hair is tied back with a headband, and she is wearing jewelry and makeup.

BRAIDED GOLD WIRE NECKLACE WITH CRESCENT-SHAPED PENDANT

RICH WOMAN'S JEWELRY
The selection of jewelry shown here would have belonged to a wealthy woman. The pieces are all made from gold and the gemstones used would have been gathered from territories all around the empire. The Romans also fashioned jewelry from bits of glass, polished to imitate genuine stones.

Hook fastener

Roman women dusted their eyelids with saffron "eyeshadow."

EARRINGS

GOLD NECKLACE WITH RED GARNET BEADS

MAKEUP FOR ROMAN WOMEN
Pale skin was desirable, so white lead was applied to the arms and face. Cheeks and lips were reddened with ochre. Antimony or black ashes went on the eyebrows and around the eyes.

Ivory comb inscribed "Modestina, farewell"

HAIRDRESSING
Like today, hair fashions came and went in the Roman world. During the early Republic, beards for men and a simple bun for women were the style. Later, clean-shaven styles for men and elaborate curls and braids for women were all the rage.

SHOPPING

IN ROMAN TOWNS, there were no supermarkets –
people went to markets or specialized shops. These
shops opened right onto the street. There were
butchers, bakers, oil shops, wine
shops, jewelers, and more.
At the end of the
day, owners shut
up their shops
by padlocking
heavy wooden
shutters to
the sidewalk.

The grain dole (free grain) was given out in the main hall.

Main street ran through the market

This terrace overlooked the forum.

Shops on first floor were cooler

Staircase

OLD MALL
The emperor
Trajan built
an enormous
shopping complex in Rome.
It had 150 shops selling
luxury goods, such as spices,
peppers, and silks from the
East, as well as ordinary fare.

MONEY AND COINAGE
At first, people paid for goods by
bartering. Later, coins were
made. During the Empire, most
coins had the emperor's head
on one side. The other side
often publicized his successes.

Hook
to hold
goods

A BAKER'S OVEN
Bakers' shops had
a mill at the back
where the flour was
ground. Dough was
made into round
flat loaves, marked
with the baker's
trademark, and
then baked in a big
oven, such as this
one from Pompeii.

STORAGE JARS
These pottery jars,
called *amphorae*, were
used to store and transport
oil, wine, and fish sauce.

STEELYARD
Traders used scales to weigh
a variety of goods. This type,
a steelyard, worked by hanging goods
from the hooks and moving a
weight along until it balanced.

ROW OF SHOPS
Shops opened early and
shut late, with a break
in the afternoon. Some
shops had signs outside
advertising what was on
sale. Goods were often
produced at the back of
the shop. Other goods
arrived by cart during
the night. Shopping
streets were dirty
and noisy places.

Workshop
making
scrolls for
writing

People lived
in rented
rooms above
the shops.

Bread was
baked in
ovens at
the back.

Butcher   Public fountain   Olive oil shop

5 9

IN THE KITCHEN

IT WAS QUITE A LUXURY to have a kitchen in Roman times. Poorer people, living in apartments, were lucky if they had a simple brazier or grill to cook on. Those who could afford to live in big houses had large, well-stocked kitchens, where industrious slaves prepared and cooked the meals. Many Roman kitchen utensils were similar to those used today, such as pots and pans, knives, sieves, ladles, and graters.

FOOD MOSAIC
Many mosaics depict food. These can give clues about what the Romans liked to eat.

MARCUS APICIUS
Apicius was a food expert. He devised many recipes – some of the strangest used nightingale tongues and camel heels! It is said he killed himself when he could no longer afford his taste for high living.

TAKEOUT
Many poor Romans had no means of cooking their own food and were forced to go out to eat. They could eat in taverns or bars, or take food to the baker's and have it cooked for them in the oven. Takeout shops, called *thermopolia*, were especially popular. They served snacks, kept hot in containers that were sunk into a counter.

Herbs were hung up to dry over the stove.

Game was hung before cooking.

Shelves held earthenware pots, dishes, and jugs.

The oil that was stored in amphorae was used for both cooking and lighting.

Stoves were fueled by wood or charcoal.

Kitchen floors were stone or decorated with mosaics.

ROMAN KITCHEN

This type of kitchen might have been found in a rich person's town house or country villa. Food was cooked in ovens or on top of charcoal on a stove. Food preparation centered around the table. Here, slaves would grind herbs and spices with a mortar and pestle, chop up meat and vegetables, and assemble eye-catching platters for dinner parties.

NO REFRIGERATORS

The Romans had no refrigerators, so perishable food such as fish and meat had to be eaten promptly, before it spoiled, or be preserved by pickling or salting.

FOOD AND EATING

THE ROMAN DIET included familiar ingredients such as meat, fish, and vegetables, although often combined in ways we might find strange today. Poor people existed mainly on a type of hot wheat and barley cereal, supplemented with vegetables – rarely meat. The first two meals of the day were

APPETIZER
Olives were popular as an appetizer. They would be followed by a glass of *mulsum* (honey wine).

often skipped. Dinner was the Romans' main meal, eaten in the afternoon. For the rich, this was a major gastronomic event that could for last hours.

Celery

Mediterranean herbs and spices

FISHY FLAVOR
Strong sauces, herbs, and spices were used to disguise the taste of meat or fish that had gone rancid. A sauce called *liquamen*, made from fish, salt, and herbs, was very popular.

PEACOCKS
The Romans ate exotic birds such as cranes, parrots, flamingoes, and peacocks. During lavish dinner parties, slaves would use the peacock feathers to fan their rich owners and brush away any flies.

Fish were kept alive in tanks to be eaten fresh.

FRESH FRUIT

Apples, pears, grapes, figs, pomegranates, dates, and plums were just some of the fruits grown across the empire. Many country estates had orchards that supplied fruit to the towns.

Fruit was improved by grafting species.

Appearance was important.

WINE

The Romans consumed a great variety of wines – sweet, dry, and honeyed. The wine was often strong and heavy, so it was mixed with water in a special mixing bowl called a *cratera*.

Decorative relief

SEATING PLAN

MEDIUS		
3	2	1

	S U M M U S
3	
2	
1	

I M U S	
1	
2	
3	

The most prestigious place to sit was at medius 3.

At a formal dinner, three couches were arranged around a square table, leaving one side free for the service. Each couch seated three people. Social status determined where people sat.

ON THE MENU

Dinner consisted of three courses: *gustatio* (appetizers such as salads and eggs), *primae mensae* (up to seven dishes of meat, fish, and poultry, such as the quail stew above), and, lastly, *secundae mensae* (fruit, nuts, and honey cakes).

EDUCATION

ONLY FORTUNATE Roman children received
an education – many poorer children had
to work as soon as they were old enough.
The lessons consisted of learning the
basics – reading, writing, and arithmetic.
There was much chanting of tables and
rote memorization. From age seven to
11 boys and girls attended elementary
school. Boys could then go on to
secondary school, but girls had
to go home and
learn housework
in preparation
for marriage.

ORATORY
If a rich man's son wanted
a political or legal career,
it was essential for him to
learn oratory, the art of
public speaking.

Brass frame

Beads in upper part
represented five times
value of lower beads

CALCULATOR
An ancient
Roman used
an abacus
to help with
addition. An
experienced user
could calculate at great
speed. The replica shown here
consists of a frame with slots. Movable
beads represent different units. This compact
type was like a pocket calculator.

PEELED PAPYRUS

SLICED REED

STRIPS PRESSED INTO PAPER

MAKING PAPYRUS PAPER

First, the outer rind of the reed was peeled. The inner part was cut into strips, soaked in water, and placed in two layers – one at right angles to the other.

The sheet was covered with linen and pressed with stones or a mallet. After drying it was polished and rolled up.

WRITING SURFACES

Over 5,000 years ago, the ancient Egyptians discovered how to make a writing surface from the papyrus plant. Only the stem was used to make papyrus rolls. Other surfaces the Romans used for writing were thin wooden tablets, bits of pottery, and parchment made from animal skin.

Papyrus grew in abundance along the banks of the Nile.

WRITING

Children learned to write using stylus pens on wax tablets (wax in a wooden frame). Romans also wrote on papyrus sheets with reed or metal pens and ink made from soot. Here is a woman with pen and wax tablet. The man holds a papyrus scroll.

Cut stem

COUNTRY LIFE

HONEYBEE
There was no sugar in ancient Rome, so people sweetened food and drinks with honey collected from beehives.

FOOD AND GOODS produced by farmworkers in the countryside fueled the great Roman towns. In the beginning, there were numerous small farmers eking out a modest living. But by the time of the Empire, much of the land had been divided into great estates, owned by wealthy Romans and staffed by slaves. Landlords spent much of the time in town, using the profits from these huge farms to finance their extravagant lifestyles.

EMMER WHEAT
Cereal crops such as emmer wheat were grown in large quantities. Grain was made into staple foods such as bread.

COUNTRY PURSUITS
Hunting was a popular country pursuit, both for sport and to obtain food. The quarries included boars, hares, deer, and game birds. Horses and special hunting dogs were sometimes used.

AN OLIVE GROVE

Olive groves could be found in many parts of the countryside. Olives were eaten as fruit, but the majority were crushed in an olive press to extract oil. The oil was stored in *amphorae* and taken to shops in towns or to ports for trading.

FRUIT AND VEGETABLES

Grapes were grown both for eating and for making into wine. Typical estates also contained fruit trees as well as vegetable gardens growing crops such as radishes, beans, cabbages, and carrots. Potatoes were unknown.

LIVESTOCK

The Romans raised various animals on their farms. Cattle and goats supplied milk; oxen drew plows; chickens, geese, and ducks provided eggs; and sheep were used for milk, wool, and meat. Pork was the most popular meat in ancient Rome.

A country estate

At the center of the country estate was the *villa*, a luxurious country house. Inside, *villas* were beautifully decorated with mosaics, fine furniture, and paintings. Outside, there were well-tended gardens, fountains, and statues. Few *villas* existed without surrounding farms. These huge estates were self-sufficient, with everything from food and wine to bakeries and bathhouses. Usually, the day-to-day running of the estate would be the job of a farm manager, who oversaw a large staff of slaves.

FLOUR MILL
Many estates had their own bakeries. Donkeys or slaves turned the flour mills.

TRANSPORTING GOODS
Carts drawn by donkeys, mules, and oxen transported produce such as grapes, olives, and vegetables from outlying fields back to the estate.

Store

Bakery

Many types of fruit were grown in the orchards.

Poultry provided eggs.

Shepherds tended sheep.

THE COUNTRY *VILLA*
There were three parts to the *villa*: the *villa urbana* was the luxurious part where the owner and family lived; the *villa rustica* housed the farm manager and laborers; and the *villa fructaria* was the storehouse for all the produce from the farm. The *villa urbana* had formal gardens in the front, and inside it was often arranged very much like a town *domus*.

TREADING GRAPES AND MAKING WINE

Slaves picked grapes from the vines, loaded them into baskets, and transported them to a special stone trough. There, slaves crushed the grapes with their bare feet. Great stone jars caught the grape juice, where it would be left to ferment.

Pottery storage jars set into the ground contained oil and wine.

Formal gardens

Private living areas

This villa urbana is two stories high with shady colonnaded porches.

Well-tended fields produced a variety of crops.

Olive press

Olive grove

Hadrian's villa

Occasionally, *villas* were built purely as luxury retreats with no working farms attached. They were often on the coast or not too far from towns. Emperor Hadrian built such a *villa* at Tivoli, near Rome. Built between A.D. 118 and 134, the *villa* extended over 300 acres (120 hectares) and contained buildings inspired by Hadrian's favorite sights from his travels around Greece and Egypt. In the grounds were bathhouses, theaters, libraries, temples, and accommodation for many guests and staff.

MARITIME THEATER
The so-called Maritime Theater is a round pool with an island in the middle, reached by a swing bridge. On the island was a pavilion thought to be Hadrian's private studio.

Emperor's palace   *Great bath*   *Canopus*

Academy

Tree-lined walkway

Circular temple

Greek theater

MODEL OF *VILLA*
This reconstruction shows the *villa* in its heyday. Buildings were sprawled over a wide area, and the grounds were landscaped with shady cypress-lined walkways and sparkling fountains. Among many wonders was a copy of the Grove of Academe where Plato tutored students

BATH VAULTS

There were two bathhouses at Hadrian's villa. Each had several sets of rooms for steaming, massage, bathing in pools, or just resting. The vaulted ceilings on the baths is a good example of Roman architectural skill.

EMPEROR HADRIAN

Born in A.D. 76, Hadrian ruled for 21 years. He was an intellectual with a passion for Greek culture. Hadrian spent much of his time traveling the provinces and visiting his armies and cultural centers such as Athens.

TEMPLE OF VENUS STATUE

The central statue is a replica of an original by Praxiteles, a Greek sculptor in the 4th century B.C.

THE CANOPUS

Hadrian made an amazing version of Canopus, an Egyptian town. He dug a large canal and imported Egyptian statues to decorate its banks. There were rows of columns joined by alternate arches and graceful caryatids (female figures used as columns).

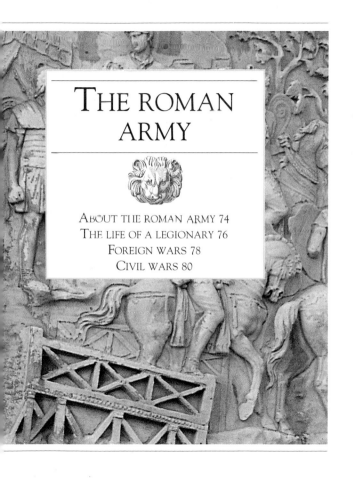

THE ROMAN ARMY

ABOUT THE ROMAN ARMY

MARCHING ACROSS THE WORLD and winning ever more lands for the empire, the Roman army was the key to Rome's success. In the early days, property-owning citizens left their farms and assembled into a part-time army during an emergency. Men supplied their own weapons. But as the frontiers of the empire widened, the army was reorganized and made permanent.

SOLDIERS OF THE REPUBLICAN ARMY
During the Republic, the army consisted of four types of soldiers. *Hastati* were young spearmen, *principes* were older, *triarii* were experienced and well armed, and *velites* (the skirmishers) were poor and lightly armed.

ARMY FACTS

• If a legion's "eagle" was captured in battle, the legion was disbanded.

• To stop enemy infiltration, each century had a password that was altered daily.

• Originally, only the rich joined the cavalry – they could afford horses.

• Hannibal's army lost 14,000 men and 25 elephants on its journey over the Alps.

PRIMA COHORS

LEGION

Cloak

Leather
bottle

The pack
weighed over
90 lb (40 kg).

Rations

Turf cutter
for making
ramparts

Wooden
frame

Mattock for
digging ditches

SOLDIER

CONTUBERNIUM

ORGANIZATION
Soldiers were grouped into legions – units of about 5,000 men. Each legion was divided into centuries of about 80 men. The centuries themselves were broken down into *contubernia*, groups of eight men. The men in each *contubernium* shared a tent and ate meals together.

MARIUS'S MULES
General Marius reformed the army. All citizens, whether rich or poor, could join. Equipment and training improved. Soldiers were called Marius's mules because of their heavy backpacks.

CENTURY

CENTURY
An experienced officer was in charge of each century. He had a special crest on his helmet so his troops could recognize him.

THE LEGION
A legion consisted of ten cohorts. A cohort was a group of centuries. The first cohort, *prima cohors*, was bigger than the rest, consisting of ten centuries. The other nine cohorts had six centuries each. Every legion carried a silver eagle standard, which was a symbol of its power.

THE LIFE OF A LEGIONARY

HARDWORKING FOOT SOLDIERS called legionaries were at the heart of the Roman army. All legionaries were Roman citizens and joined up voluntarily, swearing an oath of allegiance. They underwent tough training to make the grade. Soldiers marched for miles, carrying heavy packs loaded with vital equipment – tools for building, pots for cooking, food, and clothing. After 20-25 years of faithful service, soldiers were rewarded with money or a plot of land.

Ready to fire a stone

CATAPULT
The Romans often engaged in siege warfare. They surrounded an enemy and used battering rams and catapults to break down any defenses.

A plume or crest could be attached to top of helmet

Neck protector

ARMOR
This legionary's helmet was designed for full protection, shielding the head, cheeks, and neck without blocking out sound. A segmented metal jacket protected the chest area.

Cheek protector

Leather strips protected groin

Dagger hilt

Belt plate

Buckle

Daggers had double-edged blades.

WEAPONS

Attached to this protective belt is a short dagger, called a *pugio*. Soldiers also carried a short stabbing sword (*gladius*) and a javelin (*pilum*), which replaced spears.

Engraving of Minerva

BUILDING A FORT

Part of a legionary's training was learning about engineering, building, and surveying. Soldiers built forts, temporary camps, and defensive walls. This detail from Trajan's column shows soldiers building a fort.

Shields resemble a tortoise's shell

TORTOISE

If no other means of protection was available, soldiers formed a *testudo* (tortoise). They covered themselves with their shields, which allowed them to advance more safely.

LEG GUARDS

Officers wore metal leg protectors, called greaves, which were attached at the knee and reached to the foot. Greaves were often engraved.

FOREIGN WARS

FROM THE BEGINNING, the Romans fought wars. At first they needed to defend themselves from attackers. Later they fought with other tribes in Italy to gain control of the whole country. Once this was achieved, empire-building began in earnest. Rome's army fought on until it had conquered a huge part of the known world.

PYRRHIC WARS (280-275 B.C.)
This plate depicts a war elephant used by King Pyrrhus of Epirus, Greece, to fight the Romans for Tarentum in the south of Italy.

BOUDICCA'S REVOLT
The Celtic queen Boudicca led a revolt against the Roman army in Britain. Despite some success, she was eventually defeated.

TRIUMPHAL ARCHES
The Romans erected arches all over the empire to celebrate military victories. This arch was built in A.D. 26 at Orange in Gaul, a territory won by Julius Caesar.

PUNIC WARS
Between 264 and 146 B.C., the army fought wars with Carthage, in North Africa. The skilled Carthaginian general Hannibal crossed the Alps into Italy with elephants. After many battles, Carthage finally lost to Rome.

TRAJAN'S COLUMN
By A.D. 100, Rome
had made most of its
foreign conquests.
But emperor Trajan
added Dacia to the
empire in A.D. 106,
and he built this
ornate column to
commemorate
his victory.

GAULISH ATTACK
In 390 B.C, the Gauls
attacked the city of
Rome. Only the
Capitoline hill
survived, saved by its
sacred geese that
warned of the attack.

*When hired Numidian horsemen
changed sides to Rome,
Carthage lost.*

*Carthaginian
standard*

*Trained
battle elephant*

*These spearmen
were the only
natives in the
Carthaginian
army.*

*Spanish soldier
hired by Carthage*

*Short
stabbing
sword*

*A Roman soldier
defends himself.*

*Fierce soldiers from
Gaul wore patterned
tunics and baggy pants.*

*Celtic
mercenary
from Gaul*

CIVIL WARS

THE ARMY did not fight wars just with foreigners. During Rome's long history, there were also many internal struggles when different factions of the army fought each other. During the time of the Republic, the main civil wars were caused when two strong leaders struggled for supreme power. This eventually led to the rule of the emperors.

Dagger with double-edged blade

Belt hook

Iron scabbard

PRAETORIAN GUARD
Emperor Augustus formed an army, called the Praetorian Guard, to protect him. Highly paid and very powerful, they murdered Caligula and, against the Senate's wishes, appointed Claudius (right) as the new emperor.

ASSASSINATION WEAPON
In 49 B.C., two powerful generals, Julius Casear and Pompey, were set against each other by the Senate. Caesar defeated Pompey and became Rome's sole ruler, but he was murdered by his enemies in 44 B.C.

FOUR EMPERORS (A.D. 69)
The year following the assassination of Nero was filled with conflicts and fighting. Four different emperors held power: Galba, Otho, Vitellius, and Vespasian (shown far left).

100 miles (160 km) of crosses

Slave

SLAVE REVOLT
In 73 B.C., a gladiator called Spartacus led a slave revolt, defeating two Roman armies. The revolt was crushed in 71 B.C., and 6,000 slaves were crucified.

Rome's Appian Way

OCTAVIAN V. ANTONY
Mark Antony and Julius Caesar's nephew Octavian became allies with the aim of avenging Caesar's death. But relations between the two men collapsed, and war broke out. In 31 B.C., Antony was defeated in a sea battle. This relief depicts a warship from the period.

81

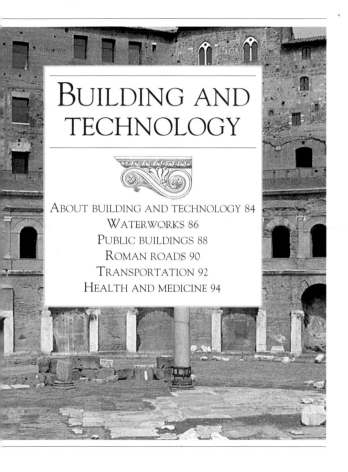

BUILDING AND TECHNOLOGY

ABOUT BUILDING AND TECHNOLOGY

MANY ROMAN BRIDGES, roads, temples, and walls built 2,000 years ago still stand today. This is a testament to the skill of the Romans, who were also masters at copying good ideas. They borrowed building styles and learned about medicine from the Greeks.

NAILS
These nails would have been used in ship-building. Many Roman tools, such as chisels and squares, look the same as those used by builders today.

Inner sanctuary

GREEK-STYLE TEMPLE
The Romans built Greek-style temples, featuring a raised podium with columns that supported a triangular pediment.

ANCIENT CRANE
This relief shows building in progress. The great wooden crane was driven by slaves walking a treadmill. Blocks of stone were tied to a pulley and then lifted by the action of the treadmill.

STURDY ARCHES
Arches had been built before, but the Romans built the most durable, using wood scaffolding to position stones or to lay concrete. Arches were featured on aqueducts, theaters, amphitheaters, and bridges.

TECHNOLOGY FACTS
• People often secretly directed water pipes into their homes to avoid paying for water.

• Roman towns were built on a grid system.

• Quack Roman doctors prescribed gladiators' blood for fertility.

• A Roman mile was about 4,790 ft (1,460 m).

HEALING THE SICK
Although Roman doctors used a variety of science-based remedies to cure the sick, people often turned to the gods for help. After a devastating plague in the third century B.C., the Romans built this temple to the god of healing, Aesculapius. People left offerings at the temple in the hope of a cure.

DOME ON THE PANTHEON
The Romans invented the dome by crossing arches over a circular area. This magnificent dome was made with concrete – another Roman invention.

A hole at the top provides light.

WATERWORKS

ROMAN CITY DWELLERS NEEDED water in vast amounts for the baths, drinking, and lavatories. To bring this water to their towns, they built aqueducts all over the empire. "Aqueduct" means carrier of water, which is exactly what they did. Channeling water from rivers, lakes, and springs, aqueducts ran underground, through mountains, and across rivers and valleys to make sure the Romans got enough water.

ARCH OF DRUSUS
First mistaken for a triumphal arch, this is part of an aqueduct.

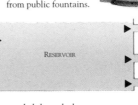

PINE CONE FOUNTAIN
Most Roman people had to collect their water from public fountains.

AQUEDUCT

RESERVOIR

PIPE

MAIN SEWER

AQUEDUCT IN ACTION
A water source had to be higher up than a town so gravity would ensure a flow. Water traveled through the aqueduct and collected in a huge reservoir. Pipes leaving the reservoir sent water to different areas, supplying public fountains, private houses (which were first to be cut off in a shortage), and the public baths. The waste ended up underground in the main sewer.

SEGOVIAN AQUEDUCT
This stone aqueduct in Segovia, Spain, was built in the early 2nd century A.D. and has 128 arches. Water was carried 98 ft (30 m) above the city along the top tier of the aqueduct.

PUBLIC LAVATORIES
Only rich households had the luxury of private facilities – most Romans used public lavatories like these. Water flowing past in a channel under the seats carried the waste away to the sewer. Like today, walls were often daubed with topical graffiti.

PUBLIC BATHS AT CLUNY, FRANCE
Huge quantities of water were needed to run the baths, a popular part of Roman life throughout the empire. Doors usually opened at midday, announced by bells, gongs, or the shouting of slaves.

Only the wealthy had a private water supply.

PRIVATE HOUSE

THE BATHS

PUBLIC FOUNTAINS

PUBLIC BUILDINGS

BUILT FROM FINE STONE such as marble, Rome's public buildings symbolized the empire's wealth and power. At the heart of every Roman city was the forum, the site of government and business buildings. In addition to these were the bathhouses, temples, theaters, and amphitheaters that were such a key part of everyday life.

THE FORUM
Similar to a town square today, the forum was the site of markets and public meetings. Clustered around the forum were many public buildings.

TRIUMPHAL ARCH
Roman emperors built triumphal arches to celebrate military victories. The emperor Constantine built this arch in A.D. 315 to celebrate his victory over his coemperor Maxentius.

Many reliefs and statues were taken from monuments of earlier emperors.

BASILICA OF CONSTANTINE AND MAXENTIUS

This huge 4th century *basilica* was the last of the great public buildings to be erected in the forum in Rome. Like all *basilicas*, it was used as law courts and for public functions.

Ceiling coffers were lined with marble.

The three barrel-vaulted aisles were used as law courts.

Constantine added main entrance in A.D. 313 after he defeated coruler Maxentius

The roof was supported by eight Corinthian columns.

TEMPLE RUIN
This temple from Rome's forum was dedicated to Castor and Pollux, mythical twin sons of the god Zeus.

RECONSTRUCTION OF THE *ROSTRA*
The forum in Rome had a public speaking platform called a *rostra*. In 44 B.C., following the death of Julius Caesar, Mark Antony used this site to make his famous speech beginning, "Friends, Romans, countrymen, lend me your ears...."

Balustrade

Honorary statue

Panel relief depicts Trajan's acts of charity

The name rostra comes from the ships' prows, seized in a sea battle, that decorated it.

ROMAN ROADS

THE ROMAN EMPIRE was vast, so a good means of traveling across it was very important. The first roads were built for military reasons: the army built roads as they conquered new lands. Roads were built as straight as possible to help the army reach troubled areas quickly. Merchants later used these roads to transport goods.

ROMAN DRAINAGE
This drain was part of a system that prevented a city's streets from getting waterlogged. Roads also had sewage and water pipes running underneath them.

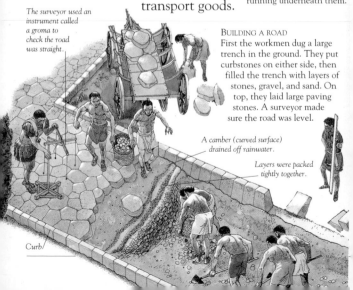

The surveyor used an instrument called a groma to check the road was straight.

BUILDING A ROAD
First the workmen dug a large trench in the ground. They put curbstones on either side, then filled the trench with layers of stones, gravel, and sand. On top, they laid large paving stones. A surveyor made sure the road was level.

A camber (curved surface) drained off rainwater.

Layers were packed tightly together.

Curb

VIA APPIA

This famous road was the first link in a network that eventually covered over 60,000 miles (96,500 km). Named after the censor Appius Claudius Caecus, who began it in 312 B.C., the Via Appia connected Rome to strategic towns and ports in the south.

Iron hobnails positioned to take soldier's weight

City streets were lined with shops and houses.

STEPPING STONES

Roads in towns had high sidewalks on either side. When the roads were wet and muddy, pedestrians used large stepping stones to cross to the other side. There were gaps between the stones for carts to drive through.

SOLDIER'S SANDALS

Each time the Roman army conquered a new city, they had a road built to it. Soldiers could march quickly along these straight, hard roads. Military sandals, called *caligae*, were strong, well ventilated, and designed to survive many long-distance marches.

TRANSPORTATION

GETTING FROM ONE PLACE to another in Rome was a time-consuming business, even along its famous straight roads. Many people traveled by foot; others went in horse-drawn coaches or two-wheeled carts. Along the route were taverns and resting places, where a traveler could stay. Milestones stood at roadsides and showed the number of miles to travel to a town.

ON HORSEBACK
The official mail was relayed by horseback. Fresh horses were provided at resting houses (*mansiones*).

FOUR-HORSE CHARIOT
Chariots were not just for the circus races. *Quadrigae* like this were used for ceremonial purposes, such as processions to celebrate military victory.

CARRIED BY LITTER
Due to traffic congestion, carts were banned from the city of Rome during the day, so the rich traveled in litters carried by slaves.

HARBOR SCENE
As trade increased around the empire, the Romans built deep harbors to serve the merchant ships that came and went. Rome was served by the port of Ostia, at the mouth of the Tiber River. These ports often grew into big towns.

Oar for steering

HORSE-DRAWN COACH
Like today's buses, coaches took a number of passengers on a journey. People sat both inside and on top. Coach journeys could be slow and uncomfortable.

Roman merchant ships had two masts.

Main sail

MERCHANT NAVY SHIP
Roman merchant ships had two masts and a hold for storing cargo. The ships were wide and sturdily built, able to transport large loads over vast distances. They could carry thousands of *amphorae* full of wine, oil, and fish sauce. Ships also transported wild animals for the arena, grain, cloth, gems, and spices.

Romulus and Remus, legendary founders of Rome

Steering sail

A lead coating prevented hull from rotting

Expertly joined planks of wood strengthened the hull.

HEALTH AND MEDICINE

ROMANS LEARNED what they knew about medicine from the Greeks. Doctors knew how to prepare soothing ointments and poultices for treating sores. They could also perform operations. But the average lifespan of a Roman was only about 40 years. Reasons for this included poor sanitation and epidemics of diseases that had no known cure.

GARLIC

FENUGREEK

MUSTARD

ELECAMPANE

FENNEL

This herb was used to settle the stomach.

SAGE

ROSEMARY

HERBAL REMEDIES
Doctors used many types of herbs and spices to make medicines. Infusions, taken internally, were made by mixing the herbs with warm water. Compresses, applied externally, were made by mashing herbs into a paste.

HEALING HERBS
Different herbs had different healing properties. For example, sage was thought to reduce fever, rosemary was prescribed for coughs, and garlic was fed to soldiers for health.

9 4

Curved tube drained bladder

SPECULUM FOR INTERNAL EXAMINATIONS

CATHETER

DOUBLE-ENDED HOOK

FORCEPS

Squeezing handles together opened prongs

MEDICINE SPOON

Hook held back sinews and veins

SURGERY
With these instruments surgeons could perform various operations. But since there were no anesthetics in ancient Rome, many people died on the operating table from the shock and pain of being cut open while awake.

RINGS
People prayed to the gods for cures. These rings depict Aesculapius, the Greek god of healing, and his daughter.

ARMY DOCTOR
The only Roman hospitals were army hospitals, solely for the treatment of wounded soldiers.

Army doctor removes arrow

VOTIVE OFFERING
Sometimes people had models made of the afflicted parts of their bodies. They left them in temples when praying for a cure, or else in gratitude if the affliction had been cured.

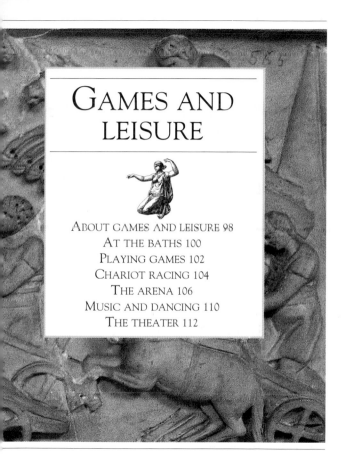

GAMES AND LEISURE

ABOUT GAMES AND LEISURE

WHEN IT CAME TO RELAXATION, the Romans had many choices. They could play games, go to the baths, or listen to music. The *ludi* (chariot racing, gladiatorial combats, and theater) drew huge crowds. These were staged by emperors or senators in honor of a god or military victory. In reality, these lavish public entertainments were used as a way of winning popularity.

MUSIC
Roman orchestras, bands, and solo musicians played a variety of wind, stringed, and percussion instruments. Here, the Greek god Pan is shown playing a lyre.

AMPHITHEATER
Gladiatorial games were staged all over the empire. This painting records a riot between Pompeiians and visiting Nucerians, in Pompeii to watch the games. An exchange of insults escalated, resulting in many deaths. Emperor Nero closed the amphitheater for ten years as a penalty.

LEISURE FACTS

• Driverless chariots could still win a race.

• Playwright Terence was once a slave.

• Trajan held games lasting 117 days.

• 50,000 people died when an amphitheater collapsed in A.D. 27.

THEATRICAL SCENERY

The theater was so much a part of life that the Romans often used theatrical decorations in their homes. This wall painting shows elaborate theatrical scenery. Going to the theater (*ludi scaenici*) was a popular pastime, especially if a comedy was on the bill. If the audience became too rowdy, the producer called for silence.

BATH GAMES

The Romans liked nothing better than a trip to the baths for a good steam, scrub, and chat. The baths were also a place for playing games – ball games and gymnastics in the yard, or, for the less energetic, board games or gambling in the shade, using dice like these.

COCKFIGHT

Many Roman leisure activities have endured to this day, including gruesome cockfights. Bets were placed and stakes were often high.

AT THE BATHS

MOST ROMAN TOWNS had at least one public bathhouse. The wealthy often had private baths in their homes. Public baths were not just places for washing – they were busy social centers, where people could exercise, chat, play games, do business, or even have their legs waxed.

Frigidarium
(*cold room*)

Tepidarium
(*warm room*)

BATH PLAN
The baths, like these at Aquae Sulis (Bath in England), consisted of a series of rooms, ranging from cold to very hot. Some had bathing pools or basins. The heat could be steamy, like a Turkish bath, or dry. On arrival, people undressed. They left their clothes in a changing room and then moved between the rooms, sweating, cooling off, and plunging into the pools.

Hypocaust

Laconicum
(*hot, dry room*)

Exercise yard
where people wrestled, lifted weights, or played games

Men and women went at different times or had separate bathhouses.

Caldarium (hot, steamy room)

Hypocaust

Carrying handle

Implements attached by rings for easy removal

Oil flask with detachable lid

The curved part of the strigil was used to scrape off dirt.

TEPIDARIUM CHANGING ROOM
Inside, the baths were often lavishly decorated. The mosaic floor of this Herculaneum *tepidarium* shows Triton surrounded by dolphins.

STRIGILS AND FLASK
The Romans did not have soap. Instead, they rubbed oil on their bodies, then scraped off the sweat, dirt, and oil with a *strigil*. At the baths, there were other health and beauty treatments available. These included massage, hairdressing, and several methods of hair removal.

HYPOCAUST SYSTEM
The floors, walls, and water were heated by a hypocaust system. An underground furnace sent hot air under floors and up through spaces behind special tiles on the walls. Floors were supported by spaced brick columns that allowed hot air to circulate easily. Water heated in a boiler above the furnace was sent to the baths through pipes.

Cold water

Hot water

Water tank

Boiler

Brick column

Space allowed air to circulate

Furnace

PLAYING GAMES

THE ANCIENT ROMANS enjoyed games. Children's toys were not very different from those of today – they included dolls, model soldiers and animals, hoops and sticks, and marbles. At the baths, in the forum, and in taverns, adults played board games with counters and gambled with dice. People of all ages enjoyed energetic ball games and athletics.

MINI CHARIOT
Only a child of wealthy parents would have had a toy like this mini goat-drawn chariot. Children's chariots were also pulled by dogs or geese.

GAMBLING COUNTERS
Counters had numbers, and sometimes names, on the back.

This means "worthless."

WINNING ATHLETE
Athletic contests were held in special stadiums. This athlete – probably a boxer – is holding a crown and a palm leaf, which was a symbol of victory.

WOMEN PLAYING
In this painting, the women are playing a dice game with knucklebones. Three knucklebones are on the ground and two are being thrown. Scores were kept for the different sides of the bones that landed face-up.

Victory palm

The size of the nuts is exaggerated in this relief.

GAME RELIEF
This relief shows children playing various throwing games. A game of nuts – marbles played with walnuts – is occupying most of the boys, although the two in the middle appear to have had a disagreement.

CHARIOT RACING

THE MOST POPULAR of the Roman games was chariot racing, or *ludi circenses*. Hordes of people gathered at the racetrack, called the circus, for a day out. Everyone had a favorite team, which they supported with the fervor of today's football fans. In Rome, each team – the Reds, Blues, Greens, and Whites – had its own stables and trainers. Champion horses also had fans.

CHARIOTEER AND HORSE
This mosaic shows a champion charioteer from the Blues team. Although most charioteers were slaves, they could acquire great wealth and prestige. Fans knew a horse's pedigree and victories by heart.

CIRCUS MAXIMUS
The Circus Maximus in Rome was the largest racetrack, holding 250,000 people. At the drop of a white cloth, the horses burst from the starting gates and thundered around the central island, or *spina*, finishing after seven laps.

TYPES OF CHARIOTS

This model shows a two-horse chariot, called a *biga*. Four-horse chariots, called *quadrigae*, were the most common. Charioteers tied the reins around their waists but carried knives so they were able to cut themselves free in the event of a crash.

Chariots were lightly built for speed.

Imperial box

AUDIENCE

All classes of Roman society enjoyed a trip to the races. The emperor and his family watched from the imperial box; others sat on tiered benches. Men and women could sit together, which made the races a popular place to meet people.

COLLISION

The most dangerous part of the race was at the turning points at either end of the central *spina*. This mosaic shows a collision. The confusion of limbs and wheels may well have meant death.

Horses were imported from the provinces, notably Spain and North Africa.

THE ARENA

THROUGHOUT THE EMPIRE people flocked to the *ludi munera* to see gladiators fight each other – and wild animals – to the death. At first, these fights were staged in the circus or in wooden arenas, but then special stone buildings, called amphitheaters, were built.

COLOSSEUM RUINS
Nearly two thousand years later, the ruins stand majestically in the center of Rome.

The Colosseum

Of all the amphitheaters built to house the games, the Colosseum in Rome was the most spectacular. Commissioned by the emperor Vespasian, the Colosseum took ten years to build and was finally opened by the emperor Titus in A.D. 80. The 50,000 people it held could be evacuated in three minutes through the 80 *vomitoria*, or exits.

NAVAL BATTLE
Built on the old site of Nero's artificial lake, the Colosseum could be flooded with water to stage mock sea battles. Gladiators fought each other from small ships.

Up to 100 ships could take part.

WILD ANIMAL FIGHT
Exotic animals were shipped in from all over the empire to fight in the arena. In games held by the emperor Trajan to celebrate his Dacian victory, 11,000 wild beasts perished.

Canopy stretched over top

Women sat high up.

The outside of the building was decorated with statues of gods.

STRUCTURE OF COLOSSEUM
The bulk of the Colosseum was supported by many arched vaults. People, carrying numbered tickets, entered through one of 80 first-floor arches and then found their way along corridors and up staircases to their seats.

WINCHING UP
Beneath the floor of the arena was a network of corridors, cells, and machinery. Here, the animals were kept in cages. When the time to fight arrived, cages were winched up to arena level, and the animals were released through a trapdoor into the arena.

Gladiator, armed with spear, prepares to fight lion

Cage opened to allow animals to climb ramp to trapdoor

Cages were like three-sided elevators.

Slaves operated the winch to lift the cage.

Gladiators

The games lasted all day; anticipation mounted when the afternoon arrived. This was when the gladiators fought. "We who are about to die salute you!" they shouted to the emperor, and the fighting began. Gladiators were usually prisoners, slaves, or criminals. Some free men thought the gladiator's life was glamorous, and they volunteered, hoping for glory. Gladiators could train at special schools, where there were masseurs, doctors, and body-building foods.

COLOSSEUM GRAFFITI
Gladiators fought one-to-one, as shown in this graffiti. A heavily armed *secutor* (left) is pitched against a lightly armed *retiarius* (right).

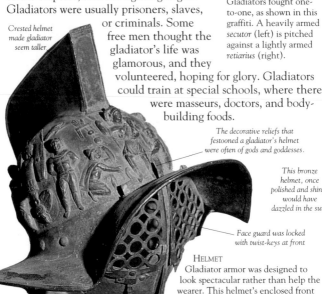

Crested helmet made gladiator seem taller

The decorative reliefs that festooned a gladiator's helmet were often of gods and goddesses.

This bronze helmet, once polished and shiny, would have dazzled in the sun.

Face guard was locked with twist-keys at front

HELMET
Gladiator armor was designed to look spectacular rather than help the wearer. This helmet's enclosed front would have given poor visibility. But, apart from perhaps arm and leg guards, this was the wearer's only protection.

Arm guard

Helmet flap to
protect neck

Vulnerable
*areas were left
*unprotected.

DIFFERENT TYPES

There were many types of gladiator.
A *retiarius* carried a net and a trident
and usually fought a *murmillo*, who wore
a fish-crowned helmet. *Thracians* had
round shields and curved daggers
and sometimes wore helmets.

RETIARIUS   MURMILLO   THRACIAN

GLADIATOR RELIEF

This relief shows two heavily armed
gladiators in combat. When wounded,
a gladiator could appeal to the crowd
for mercy. Thumbs up meant mercy
granted, thumbs down meant death.

WINNING GLADIATOR

Successful gladiators became stars. Many
victories could bring fame, fortune, and
freedom from slavery. Freed gladiators
often set up their own gladiator schools.

MUSIC AND DANCING

THE SOUND OF MUSIC rang through the Roman world. Music was played at the theater, gladiatorial games, dinner parties, in the streets, and during funeral processions and religious ceremonies. Musicians were usually freedmen or slaves. The nobility often took music and dance lessons, but they never performed professionally, since to do this was considered vulgar.

Ornate handle

SISTRUM
This instrument worked like a rattle. The player held it by the handle and shook it, causing the bronze bars to jingle.

CORNU
Wind instruments were popular in ancient Rome. This long, curved horn, called a cornu, was sometimes used by the army for signaling.

TRAVELING BAND
Bands of musicians traveled around and performed in the streets. This mosaic shows a child with a flute, a tambourine player, and a dancer holding cymbals. The masked figure is playing double pipes – two pipes with reed mouthpieces, which were played simultaneously.

FUNERAL DANCERS
Dance was an important part of some religious ceremonies. This tomb painting shows the dance of the mourners – a group of women, wearing long, hooded cloaks, skip sideways, arms linked.

CONCERT
This wall painting shows four women practicing music for a concert. A group like this, along with dancers, and perhaps acrobats, jugglers, and conjurers, might have entertained dinner party guests. The seated woman is playing a lyre. Its strings are plucked with fingers or a plectrum, causing the tortoiseshell soundbox to resonate.

Cymbals were often used in religious ceremonies.

Handhold

Linked together by chain

CYMBALS
Like their modern equivalent, these bronze cymbals were played by crashing them together. Cymbals were joined either by a rope, a piece of leather, or a chain.

THE THEATER

THE ROMANS adopted the idea of theater from the Greeks. At first, translations of Greek plays were performed. Later, original plays were written by Roman playwrights such as Plautus and Terence. Comedies were preferred to tragedies. Mime was a Roman invention, but, unlike today's mime, actors spoke!

THEATER RUINS
The Romans built theaters all over the empire, like this theater of Aspendus in Asia Minor.

IN THE WINGS
In this mosaic a group of actors are preparing for a play. Two actors are practicing dance steps, one actor is being helped into his costume, and a musician is playing double pipes. Masks lie ready to be worn at the performance.

Poorer people sat higher up.

Underneath the seats, a network of corridors and stairs allowed easy exit.

THEATER PLAN

Roman theater design followed that of the Greeks, with some changes. Both were a D-shape, with tiers of seats. But the seats in Roman theaters were often supported by arches and vaults, rather than cut into the slope of a hillside. The first wooden theaters were later replaced by sturdier ones of stone.

MASKS

Theaters were very big, so actors wore masks to help the audience recognize the various types of characters. Masks could denote happy and tragic figures, male and female, and young and old. Male characters wore brown masks; females wore white. Special devices were built into the masks to help the actors project their voices.

The stone background on the stage was elaborately decorated.

A canvas velarium could be pulled over these poles to keep the sun off the audience.

The orchestra was the area situated in front of the stage.

The scenery could be changed using special machinery.

Hoists that lifted actors from the stage, trapdoors, and other tricks provided special effects.

A curtain fell to the floor to reveal the stage.

Arches supported the seats.

RELIGION, FESTIVALS, AND DEATH

ABOUT RELIGION, FESTIVALS, AND DEATH

THE ROMANS BELIEVED in gods, goddesses, and life after death. They adopted some of the Greek gods and merged the personalities of others with the existing Roman "state gods." There were also many lesser gods and spirits, and as the Romans conquered new lands they tended to absorb the new religions they encountered. Many festivals were held in honor of the gods.

GREEK GOD
Rome had no god similar to Greek Apollo, so they adopted him. He was god of the Sun and of prophecy. This is a Roman reproduction of a Greek statue.

ROMAN TEMPLES
Temples were built all over the empire and dedicated to different gods. They were also dedicated to emperors, who were often worshiped as gods. This temple in Rome, called the Pantheon, was built in honor of all the gods.

THE SACRIFICIAL ALTAR

At an altar outside the temple, offerings were made to the gods to keep them happy and to ask them for favors. Only priests could perform these complicated rituals because people believed the gods would not accept a sacrifice if a mistake was made.

Altar

SACRIFICE

Pigs, oxen, and many other animals died on the sacrificial altar during religious ceremonies. Animals were usually white, but black animals were offered to gods of the underworld.

FOREIGN GOD

Mithras was a Persian god, very popular with soldiers. Although the cult of Mithraism was in favor of equality, women were barred from joining the religion.

Bull's blood was held to be life-giving.

Mithras slays bull

THINKING ABOUT DEATH

This strange mosaic from Pompeii shows a skull with a measuring instrument. Its message is that death is a certainty, so life should be enjoyed, because death is the great leveler and gives a true measure of all things.

WORSHIP AND BELIEFS

THERE WERE NO CHURCH SERVICES in Rome – people took offerings to temples if they had a favor to ask a god. They also prayed daily at the household shrine. Worship consisted of processions, praying, and making sacrifices. During imperial times, many turned to foreign gods, who offered novelty and more involvement in religious ceremonies.

This temple was built in the 2nd century B.C.

GOOD AND BAD SIGNS
Romans looked for signs in the natural world. Priests examined animal innards or observed bird flight and cloud formation for omens. If sacred chickens ate hungrily, the gods were happy.

TEMPLE OF PORTUNUS, GOD OF RIVERS AND PORTS
Inside each Roman temple was a statue of the god or goddess to whom the temple was dedicated. People would visit the temple of their favorite god with offerings and pray privately for special needs.

CULT OF VESTA

Vesta was the Roman goddess of the hearth and household. Her shrine in Rome's forum was served by six women called the Vestal Virgins. Their task was to keep the shrine's sacred fire alight. They came from noble families and served Vesta for 30 years. The Vestal Virgins could not marry.

Temple of Vesta

Inner chamber

Sacred flame

Ring of Corinthian columns

WHICH GOD?

People would pray to different gods to ask for different favors. Venus was the goddess of love, beauty, and fertility.

MAKING A SACRIFICE

As the priest and his assistants performed the ritual sacrifice, a piper played a tune to drown any sounds of ill omen. The animal's internal organs were burned on the altar, and liquids such as wine were poured over to create a lot of smoke.

HOUSEHOLD GODS

Each house had a shrine, or *lararium*. The gods who looked after a house were called *lares* and *penates*.

GODS AND GODDESSES

THE ROMANS WORSHIPED many gods and
goddesses. These were seen as larger-than-
life humans. They had their good and bad
points, but unlike humans they lived forever.
The state gods had the same personalities
as their Greek counterparts but different
names. Foreign gods
were entirely different.

BACCHUS
This was the god of
wine and revelry. His
festivals were usually
wild, drunken occasions.

*Grapes, the
symbol of
wine*

*Mars was
the Roman
god of war.*

*Gilded
silver*

MARS ALATOR
The local gods of subject
peoples often became
merged with the Roman
state gods. This temple
offering from Britain
was dedicated to a
"mixed" god called
Mars Alator.

CYBELE
A mother
goddess and
originally from
Turkey, Cybele
became part of
the Roman state
religion. These
clamps may have
had a gruesome use
sometimes Cybele's
priests would castrate
themselves for her.

120

Detail from triumphal arch

Jupiter was god of the sky.

Busts of gods decorate clamps

Bronze handle

Head of a lion

VICTORY
This winged figure personified success in battle. She often appeared on buildings erected to celebrate military victory.

JUPITER
Known by the Romans as greatest and best, Jupiter was the king of the gods. His symbols were an eagle and a thunderbolt.

Anubis prepares body for afterlife

JACKAL-HEADED ANUBIS
Anubis was the Egyptian god of mummification. Many people in Roman Egypt adopted Egyptian burial practices and were mummified after death.

FESTIVALS

THROUGHOUT THE YEAR the Romans celebrated many festivals. Most of them were religious, in honor of a certain god or goddess. Festivals were celebrated in a variety of ways. There were processions to the temple to offer up sacrifices. Festival goers also enjoyed eating, drinking, music and dancing, and lively public entertainments.

Vestal Virgin

MARCH 1
This was the day when the Vestal Virgins lit a new fire to the goddess Vesta at her shrine in the Roman forum.

SATURNALIA (DECEMBER 7-14)
The biggest festival of the year was held in honor of Saturn, god of agriculture. The Romans exchanged presents and gave dinner parties with a difference: masters waited on the slaves.

FLORALES (APRIL 28–MAY 3)
This colorful festival was held in honor of
Flora, the goddess of flowers. People wore
garlands of fresh flowers on their
heads and around their
necks and celebrated
by dancing.

Wild rose

PARENTALIA (FEBRUARY 13-21)
During this festival people
honored their dead parents.
Temples closed down, and
weddings were
forbidden.

*People visited the
tombs of their parents.*

JANUARY 1
On this day
new consuls were
sworn in at the Senate.
Bulls were sacrificed to
Jupiter to thank him
for his protection
during the past year.

SOME OTHER FESTIVALS
• February 15 – feast of
the founding of Rome
(*Lupercalia*): runners
raced around Palatine
hill, whipping spectators
with goat skins.

• March 15 – festival of
Anna Perenna: Romans
picnicked by the Tiber.

• August 13 – feast of
Diana, moon goddess:
slaves had a day off.

DEATH AND BURIAL

THE RICH WERE TREATED very differently from the poor in death. A deceased noble lay in state in the *atrium*. A procession took the body through the streets on a litter, a speech was made, and a banquet held at the family tomb. The poor were often buried in common pits in public cemeteries.

Inscription says urn holds the remains of an "unfortunate mother"

BURIAL URNS
Cremation was popular for a long time in Rome. The ashes of the dead person were first washed with wine or water and then placed in an urn.

Glass urn

Marble urn

Passersby read inscriptions and remembered the dead.

All the family were expected to stand by and mourn.

Child lies on her deathbed

Last dying breath was caught by nearest relative, who also closed dead person's eyes

TRIP TO THE UNDERWORLD

Wealthy people could afford to have commemorative scenes (above) carved on their tombs. Most Romans believed that the dead were ferried across the Styx River to Hades (the Underworld). Mourners would put a coin in the dead person's mouth to pay the ferryman.

FUNERAL GAMES

The "games" in which gladiators fought each other to the death probably began as funeral games. Staged by nobles in honor of their dead relatives, these gladiatorial combats were looked on as a status symbol. The more flamboyant the show, the better this reflected on the host.

Tombs like these once lined the Via Appia outside Rome.

Some tombs looked like miniature temples.

ROAD OF TOMBS

Burial grew popular in the 2nd century A.D. By law, bodies were buried beyond city limits – partly to stop disease. Tomb-lined roads existed outside most towns.

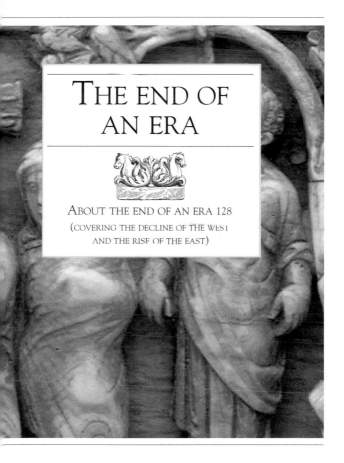

THE END OF
AN ERA

ABOUT THE END OF AN ERA 128
(COVERING THE DECLINE OF THE WEST
AND THE RISE OF THE EAST)

ABOUT THE END OF AN ERA

THE ROMAN EMPIRE ENJOYED PEACE and prosperity for over 200 years. But by the start of the 3rd century A.D., cracks were beginning to show. Such a large empire was difficult to manage and needed a strong leader. However, after the death of Marcus Aurelius (A.D. 180), there was conflict at the top, attacks on Rome's frontiers, and economic crisis.

This short, double-edged sword was a very effective stabbing weapon.

Baldric
(shoulder belt)

PERSECUTION OF CHRISTIANS
Many blamed Rome's demise on Christians, thinking they had angered the state gods by refusing to worship them. Roman Christians buried their dead in these underground chambers.

RULED BY THE SWORD
The death of Marcus Aurelius marked the beginning of a period when army generals fought each other for control. Over a span of 80 years, more than 40 different emperors came to power. Some only ruled a few months; many were killed.

Scabbard made from wood covered in leather and decorated in bronze

128

- Emperor Diocletian increased the Roman army from 300,000 to 450,000 soldiers.
- Emperor Julian, the nephew of Christian emperor Constantine, tried to restore the pagan religion.
- Some Barbarians adopted Roman ways.

CLASPED HANDS
When two emperors coruled, this symbol often appeared on coins as propaganda to reassure people they got along.

BARBARIANS
Tribes known by the Romans as Barbarians began to attack the frontiers of the empire, especially along the Rhine and Danube rivers. The Romans allowed some to settle in the empire in return for their help in defending against any further invasion.

The Barbarians were skilled metalworkers.

Gemstones

VISIGOTH BRONZE EAGLE-SHAPED BROOCH

CONVERSION TO CHRISTIANITY
In 312, emperor Constantine saw a flaming cross in the sky before he fought the usurper Maxentius for control of Rome. Constantine was convinced he owed his victory to God. This ended the persecution of Christians. Christianity was later to become the state religion.

The decline of the West

In A.D. 286 emperor Diocletian decided that the Roman empire was too big to be ruled by just one person. He appointed a coemperor and two junior emperors. Diocletian ruled the eastern part of the empire, while his coemperor, Maximian, ruled in the West. The East and West faced very different fates. Over the following 200 years the power of the western part of the Roman empire steadily declined.

The Romans depicted death as a reminder to enjoy life.

Water pitcher

SKELETON MOSAIC

THE RICH GET RICHER

There had been a gradual polarization of wealth. While the rich gave lavish dinner parties, the poor could hardly afford to eat. Heavily taxed and stripped of many legal rights, the poor lost faith in the empire. Many preferred life under the barbarian invaders.

DEATH

Plagues raged through the western provinces, killing thousands of people. This meant that the empire had fewer workers, fewer slaves, and fewer soldiers.

Gesture of
harmony

Egyptian
coin

ECONOMIC DECLINE
Prices spiraled upward. Between
A.D. 200-280 the price of a bale
of wheat in Egypt rose from 16
drachmas to 120,000 drachmas.

FARMERS
The cost of defending the empire
was high and taxes were raised.
Many farmers abandoned their
farms because they could not
afford to pay.

Farmers deserted
their fields and
became brigands.

Eagle
symbolizes
Roman empire

DIOCLETIAN
This emperor was a general,
chosen by his army. He restored order and
ensured the empire was run more efficiently,
but his policies were very harsh. This statue,
showing him, his coruler, and their two assistants
as one, was meant to stress the unity of their rule.

131

The rise of the East

While the western half of the Roman empire declined, the eastern part of the empire flourished. Byzantium was rebuilt into the glittering city of Constantinople, replacing Rome as the capital of the empire. Out of the dying embers of the old, a new empire rose that was to last for another thousand years. Its people spoke Greek instead of Latin. We call it the Byzantine empire, named after the Greek city that was its birthplace.

CONSTANTINE
In 330 this emperor moved the empire's capital to Byzantium and renamed the city Constantinople.

THE ROMAN EMPIRE AT A.D. 330

VISIGOTHS SACK CITY OF ROME
Barbarian tribes had been allowed to penetrate the frontiers of the empire, and the Romans had become dependent on them for help with defense. But waves of attacks followed, and in 410 King Alaric of the Visigoths sacked Rome itself. It was the first time the city had been conquered for 800 years.

Barbarians used battleaxes.

THE END
The West survived for a time after the sack of Rome, but in 476 the last western emperor, Romulus Augustulus, was deposed by Odoacer, a German general.

Central dome

Marble
and mosaic
interior

In 1453 the church
became a mosque.

Buildings were pillaged
and burned.

Visigoths rampaged
through the streets
for three days.

Christian King
Alaric ordered his
men not to steal
Christian objects.

Some Goths
had served as
auxiliaries in the
Roman army.

Cameo set in
ornately
worked
gold

HAGIA SOPHIA (CHURCH OF HOLY WISDOM)
Eastern emperor Justinian (ruled 527-65)
reconquered lands that the Barbarians had
conquered in Africa, Italy, and Spain. He
also brought all the Roman laws together
in a book. In Constantinople he built
Hagia Sophia, which was the largest
church in the Christian world.

BYZANTINE ART
Art, trade, and culture thrived in the new
Byzantine empire. Its capital, Constantinople,
ideally located between Europe and Asia, grew
wealthy. Lavish mosaics decorated buildings,
and the rich wore jewels like this gold brooch.

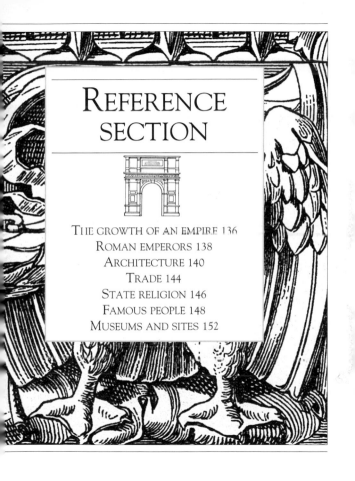

REFERENCE SECTION

THE GROWTH OF AN EMPIRE

THE VAST AREA known as the Roman empire was the result of many centuries of warfare. From a small city founded on the banks of the Tiber River in Italy, Rome grew into a powerful empire that stretched from the Atlantic Ocean in the west to the Euphrates River in the east, and from Hadrian's Wall in the north to the Sahara Desert in the south.

PHASES OF EXPANSION
Rome's growth began with the gradual conquest of Italy. By the late 1st century B.C., Rome was ruler of every Mediterranean shore. The fall of Dacia (now Romania) in A.D. 106 brought the empire to its greatest extent.

EMPIRE AT 264 B.C.

EMPIRE AT 201 B.C.

EMPIRE AT 30 B.C.

EMPIRE AT A.D. 117

North Sea

LONDINIUM (LONDON)

Atlantic Ocean

NARBO (NARBONN

TARRACO (TARRAGONA)

SEGOVIA (SEGOVIA)

CARTHAGO NOVA (CARTAGENA)

GADES (CADIZ)

Sahara Desert

AFRICA

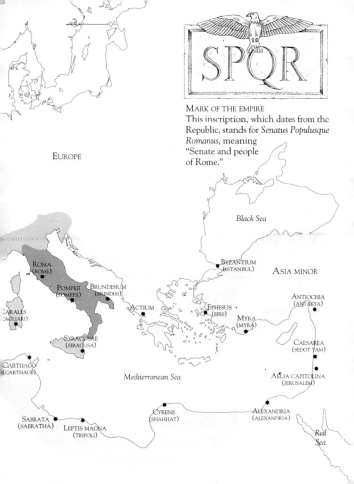

EUROPE

MARK OF THE EMPIRE
This inscription, which dates from the Republic, stands for *Senatus Populusque Romanus*, meaning "Senate and people of Rome."

Black Sea

ASIA MINOR

ROMA
(ROME)

POMPEII
(POMPEII)

BRUNDISIUM
(BRINDISI)

ACTIUM

EPHESUS
(EFES)

MYRA
(MYRA)

ANTIOCHIA
(ANTAKYA)

CARALES
(CAGLIARI)

SYRACUSAE
(SIRACUSA)

CAESAREA
(SEDOT YAM)

CARTHAGO
(CARTHAGE)

Mediterranean Sea

AELIA CAPITOLINA
(JERUSALEM)

SABRATA
(SABRATHA)

LEPTIS MAGNA
(TRIPOLI)

CYRENE
(SHAHHAT)

ALEXANDRIA
(ALEXANDRIA)

BYZANTIUM
(ISTANBUL)

Red Sea

ROMAN EMPERORS

THE CIVIL WARS that followed the death of Julius Caesar brought the period known as the Republic to an end.

Augustus	31 B.C.-AD. 14
Tiberius	14-37 A.D.
Caligula (Gauis)	37-41
Claudius	41-54
Nero	54-68
Galba	68-69
Otho	69
Vitellius	69
Vespasian	69-79
Titus	79-81
Domitian	81-96
Nerva	96-98
Trajan	98-117
Hadrian	117-138
Antoninus Pius	138-161
Marcus Aurelius	161-180
Lucius Verus	161-169
Commodus	177-192
Pertinax	193
Didius Julianus	193
Septimius Severus	193-211
Caracalla	198-217
Geta	209-212
Macrinus	217-218
Elagabalus	218-222
Severus Alexander	222-235
Maximinus I	235-238
Gordian	238
Gordian II	238
Pupienus	238
Balbinus	238
Gordian III	238-244
Philip	244-249
Decius	249-251
Hostilian	251
Gallus	251-253
Aemilian	253
Valerian	253-260
Gallienus	253-268
Claudius II Gothicus	268-270
Quintillus	269-270
Aurelian	270-275
Tacitus	275-276
Florian	276
Probus	276-282
Carus	282-283
Carinus	283-285
Numerian (co-emperor)	283-284

Octavian, Caesar's adopted son, won the struggle for power. He restored normal government in 27 B.C. and was given the name Imperator Caesar Augustus. *Imperator* meant "victor in battle" and is the origin of the word emperor.

NOT A KING
Emperors wore wreaths of laurel rather than crowns.

GALLIC REBEL STATES	
Postumus	260-269
Victorinus	269-271
Tetricus	271-274

Weak emperors led to the creation of rebel states. The kingdom of Palmyra in the East and the "Gallic empire" of Gaul, Britain, and Spain were finally defeated by the emperor Aurelian.

EASTERN REBEL STATE OF PALMYRA	
Zenobia	266-272
(Joint ruler with her son Vaballath)	

Diocletian	285-286

WESTERN EMPIRE

Maximian	286-305
Constantius I	305-306
Severus	305-307
Maxentius (usurper)	307-312
Constantine I	307-324

EASTERN EMPIRE

Diocletian	286-305
Galerius	305-311
Maximinus II	310-313
Licinius	308-324

Constantine I (sole emperor)	324-337

Constantine II	337-340
Constans	337-350
Magnentius	350-353

Constantius II	337-361
(Sole emperor after defeating Magnentius in 353 – again the empire was briefly reunited)	

Julian	361-363
Jovian	363-364

Valentinian I	364-375
Gratian	375-383
Valentinian II	375-392
Honorius	395-423
Johannes	423-425
Valentinian II	425-455
Petronius Maximus	455
Avitus	455-456
Majorian	457-461
Libius Severus	461-467
Anthemius	467-472
Olybrius	472
Glycerius	473-474
Julius Nepos	474-475
Romulus Augustulus	475-476

Valens	364-378
Procopius	365-366
Theodosius I	379-395
Arcadius	395-408
Theodosius II	400-450
Marcian	450-457
Leo I	457-474
Leo II	474
Zeno	474-491

THE EAST SURVIVES
In A.D. 476 the last western emperor lost his power, but the eastern (or Byzantine) empire lived on until 1453.

ARCHITECTURE

MUCH OF ROMAN ARCHITECTURE was influenced by the Greeks, but the Romans did make innovations of their own. Massive arched aqueducts brought water to the towns, where much of daily life was centered around the fine public buildings of the forum, or town square.

DOMES

The dome was a feature of Roman architecture that the Greeks never employed. This construction was a Roman invention. With its use, together with arches and vaults, the distinctive style of the interior of Roman buildings began to evolve.

CROSS-SECTION

A domed roof is constructed by crossing a series of arches over each other, as this cross-section shows.

PANTHEON

The most impressive example of a dome is the Pantheon, made possible by the Roman invention of concrete.

Concrete cast with hollowed panels to reduce weight

ARCHES

The use of the arch is a fundamental feature of Roman architecture. The Greeks and the Etruscans also built arches but did not use them in as many different ways. Before the Romans, most buildings were supported by columns and walls. Roman architects were able to build across greater distances because arches can support much heavier loads.

AQUEDUCTS

These consisted of a series of arches on several levels. The water channel at the top maintained a constant gradient.

THEATERS

The tiered seating in Roman theaters was supported by arches. The Greeks built their theaters on natural slopes.

BRIDGES

Arched bridges could stretch across rivers and valleys. The hills on either side acted as buttresses, or supports.

TRIUMPHAL ARCHES

This type of arch had no practical function. The Romans built triumphal arches to celebrate victory in battle.

AMPHITHEATERS

Tiered arches supported the rows of seating, which completely encircled the amphitheater's central arena.

141

VAULTS

These structures would have been difficult to build without the use of concrete. Vaults were built by placing a line of arches side by side to make a tunnel shape. Based on this model, different types of vault evolved.

GROIN VAULT

Crossing two barrel vaults at right angles to each other formed the groin vault.

BARREL VAULT

This tunnel-like structure was the original type the Romans used.

CEILING

Groin vaults were first used in the Roman baths, as shown here in the Baths of Diocletian.

COLUMNS

The Romans used five types of columns in their temples and other public buildings, borrowing the three classic orders – Doric, Ionic, and Corinthian – from the Greeks.

Capital

TUSCAN

Capitals of this order are like the Doric, but the columns are plain, not fluted.

COMPOSITE

The capitals are similar to the Corinthian but with Ionic-style motifs.

DORIC   IONIC   CORINTHIAN

ORNAMENTATION

The Romans were noted for decorating their public buildings with many intricate motifs. Unlike the Greeks, who concentrated on exterior ornamentation, Roman buildings were just as lavishly decorated on the inside. Richly carved columns were often erected for decorative rather than structural purposes. Ornate friezes were another popular feature of Roman architecture.

FRIEZE
This section from a Roman frieze depicts an entwined foliage design, which is then repeated. These decorative panels were also used to record events or tell a story.

ANTEFIX

A finial (bunch of foliage) design was often used as an antefix – a type of decoration that concealed the ends of roofing tiles.

ROSETTE

This rosette from the Forum of Nerva is made of acanthus leaves, a popular design and a characteristic of Corinthian capitals.

CAPITAL

Ionic columns were decorated with twin spiral designs on either side of the capitals.

TEMPLES

Roman temples looked very like Greek ones – oblong in shape, with a triangular pediment over the entrance. There were usually rows of columns at the front and sides (a peristyle). Temples were built on a platform to make them stand out from other buildings in the town. A statue of the temple god was kept in an inner sanctuary.

Columns

Triangular pediment

Only priests entered inner sanctuary

Ceremonies took place at altar in front of temple

TRADE

THE TRADING NETWORK of the Roman empire was vast and thriving. The provinces supplied Rome with a huge variety of goods; they also traded with each other. For a long time, there was peace throughout the lands and seas of the empire, so traders were safe to travel without fear of attack from bandits or pirates.

COMMODITY		ORIGIN (PRESENT-DAY LOCATION)
	Gold, silver, iron, copper, tin, lead	Spain had numerous mines. Britain, France, Cyprus, Turkey, and parts of central Europe exported metals.
	Fruit, fish, grain, salt	Egypt, Spain, N. Africa (main grain producers); Romania (salt); Mediterranean areas (fish and fruit).
	Honey	Greece was the main producer of honey within the empire. It was also imported from the Ukraine.
	Olive oil	The principal oil producers were Spain, N. Africa, Italy, Greece, Syria, and Turkey.
	Wine	Italy, Sicily, Spain, France, Turkey, the Greek Islands, and Syria were the main wine producers.
	Lumber, marble	Greece, N. Africa, Turkey, Italy (marble); N. Africa, Lebanon, Turkey (lumber).

COMMODITY		ORIGIN (PRESENT-DAY LOCATION)
	Drugs, herbs	Egypt and N. Africa were the main exporters of drugs. Many herbs were grown in the Mediterranean regions.
	Purple dye	N. Africa, Israel, Lebanon, and Greece all produced this dye, which was distilled from murex seashells.
	Wool, textiles	Britain, Spain, Turkey, Syria, Greece, France, and Italy were exporters of these products.
	Glass, pottery	Greece, France, Germany, Spain, N. Africa, Turkey, and Italy all exported a range of these products.
	Horses, wild animals for the arena	Coastal towns in N. Africa and Egypt exported wild animals. Romania, Spain, and N. Africa supplied horses.
	Precious stones	Turkey exported emeralds. Most precious stones were imported into the empire from farther east.
	Leather, hides	These goods were mostly obtained from northern parts of the empire, such as Britain and the Danube lands.
	Ivory	Ivory was transported from central Africa and imported into the empire via the Red Sea
	Papyrus	Papyrus grew in abundance along the banks of the Nile River. Egypt was the only exporter.

STATE RELIGION

THE ROMANS WORSHIPED state gods and goddesses. This "family" of gods included husbands, wives, mothers, fathers, and children, who all had human characteristics such as jealousy. These Roman gods were very similar to the god family worshiped by the Greeks, and the Greek counterpart is given here after the name of each Roman god.

JUNO (HERA)
Mother of war god Mars, Juno protected women, especially in childbirth.

JUPITER (ZEUS)
King of the gods, Jupiter controlled the skies and all celestial phenomena. Places struck by lightning were walled off and made his property. He married his sister Juno, but was forever unfaithful to her.

MINERVA (ATHENA)
She was the goddess of wisdom, crafts, and war.

AUGUSTUS
He was the first of many emperors to be deified.

DIS (PLUTO)
God of the underworld,
Dis was greatly feared.

NEPTUNE (POSEIDON)
The sea god rode a gold
chariot with white horses.

VESTA (HESTIA)
Bright and pure, she was
goddess of the hearth.

VENUS (APHRODITE)
Born from sea foam, she
was the goddess of love.

MARS (ARES)
This god of war was
the father of Romulus.

DIANA (ARTEMIS)
Moon and hunting deity,
her arrows brought plague.

APOLLO (APOLLO)
He was god of the Sun
and a patron of the arts.

MERCURY (HERMES)
This messenger of the gods
had winged sandals and hat.

BACCHUS (DIONYSUS)
Wine god Bacchus led a
band of merry revelers.

FAMOUS PEOPLE

THE ROMANS LEFT BEHIND a rich legacy in literature, language, architecture, and laws. Poets, writers, historians, political leaders, scientists, architects, and many others played a role in shaping and preserving this legacy.

BOUDICCA (DIED A.D. 60)
Queen of the Iceni tribe in Roman Britain, Boudicca led a revolt against Roman rule in A.D. 60. The rebels wreaked havoc throughout eastern England and, according to Tacitus, killed 70,000 Romans and their British supporters. Britain's governor, Suetonius Paulinus, finally crushed the revolt. Boudicca probably killed herself.

CICERO (106-43 B.C.)
Marcus Tullius Cicero was a politician, scholar, lawyer, and writer. Educated in Rome and Greece, he became a great orator. Many of his speeches and writings have survived. He was in favor of the Republic and opposed Julius Caesar's dictatorship. He was later murdered for speaking out against the government.

CLEOPATRA (69-30 B.C.)
Cleopatra became queen of Egypt in 51 B.C. She was of Greek descent, but she spoke Egyptian and considered herself daughter of the Egyptian Sun god, Ra. Cleopatra was no beauty, but she did possess great charm, and she used this to seduce two great Romans: Julius Caesar and Mark Antony. This was probably more to enhance her power than for love. After Octavian defeated Antony at the Battle of Actium, both Antony and Cleopatra committed suicide.

COLUMELLA

Lucius Columella was born in Spain. He served as a tribune and fought in Syria. Columella was very interested in agriculture and wanted to find ways to improve production. In about A.D. 60 he wrote a set of farming textbooks in which he gave advice on *villas*, farm buildings, crops, and types of soil. His books were read avidly by many Roman landowners.

JUVENAL (c. A.D. 60-136)

This poet wrote about Roman life in works called satires. These are writings that criticize people's shortcomings and evils by poking fun at them. Juvenal attacked many things about life in the city, including the indiscretions of Roman society people and poor housing conditions. He described Rome as "a city that's propped up with little more than matchsticks."

LIVY (59 B.C.-A.D. 17)

Titus Livius, known to us as Livy, was a historian. He also tutored the young Claudius, future emperor. Livy's history of Rome, called "Books from the Founding of Rome," filled 142 books, but only 35 have survived. The history began at the dawn of Rome and was used as a textbook in Roman schools.

MARTIAL (c. A.D. 40-104)

Born in Spain, this poet liked to claim he was descended from Celts and Iberians. However, he was a freeborn Roman citizen and spent most of his life in Rome under the patronage of various aristocratic families. Martial invented the epigram, a type of poem with a witty ending. He wrote about everyday life and the leading individuals of Roman society.

PLAUTUS (c.254-184 B.C.)

This playwright wrote many plays, but only 21 have survived. Like other Roman dramatists, he based his plays on Greek comedies, but he introduced aspects of Roman life to make them more appealing to Roman audiences. Plautus influenced later writers, especially Shakespeare, who used Plautus's plots in some of his own plays.

PLINY THE ELDER (A.D. 23-79)

Admiral Pliny (as he was also known) commanded a fleet of warships. He died in the Vesuvius eruption when he sailed across the Bay of Naples in a bid to rescue trapped people. He wrote *Historiae Naturalis*, a natural history work in 37 volumes, which dealt with plant-based medicines, as well as anatomy.

PLINY THE YOUNGER (c.A.D. 61-113)

Gaius Pliny was eyewitness to the Vesuvius disaster that killed his uncle. Pliny the Younger trained as a lawyer. He served as a provincial governor, writing many letters to emperor Trajan. He also wrote to his friend Tacitus and others. His letters are full of information about events in the Roman world.

SENECA (c.4 B.C.-A.D. 65)

Seneca was born in Cordoba, Spain, but lived most of his life in Rome as a philosopher, poet, and lawyer. In A.D. 41 he was charged with adultery and banished to Corsica by emperor Claudius. He was later tutor and adviser to emperor Nero. Seneca retired because he was repulsed by the emperor's crimes. He was later accused of plotting against Nero and committed suicide.

SUETONIUS (c. A.D. 69-140)

Historian Gaius Suetonius Tranquillus was a friend of Pliny the Younger. He wrote several books. The most famous, called "Lives of the Twelve Caesars," is about Roman rulers from Julius Caesar to Domitian. It contains many scandalous and amusing anecdotes about these rulers' private lives.

TACITUS (c. A.D. 56-117)

Senator Cornelius Tacitus was a great Roman historian. His distinguished political career was probably aided by his marriage to General Agricola's daughter. He served as *proconsul* of Asia, the top provincial posting. His most famous published works are "The Histories" (the Roman empire from A.D. 69 to 96) and "The Annals" (A.D. 14-68: Rome's emperors from Tiberius to Nero).

VITRUVIUS (BORN c. 70 B.C.)

The architect and engineer Vitruvius wrote a guide for architects called "De Architectura," which covered different types of structures, like theaters and buildings in the forum. His guide also gave information on town planning and construction. Vitruvius was opposed to "modern" architecture, preferring the classic-style temples and public buildings.

ZENOBIA

Queen of the Roman colony of Palmyra in present-day Syria, Zenobia was not content with ruling under Roman control. She conquered Egypt in A.D. 269 and took most of Asia Minor in 270, declaring independence from Rome. Emperor Aurelian finally defeated Zenobia in 272 and took her to Rome, parading her in his triumphal procession. She went on to marry a senator and lived the rest of her life at their *villa* outside the city of Rome.

MUSEUMS AND SITES

THE FOLLOWING is only a partial list of museums and sites where ancient Roman artifacts and building remains can be seen. Many more exist throughout Europe, the Middle East, and North Africa.

Museums
(and useful addresses)

UNITED STATES

American Academy in Rome
667 Madison Avenue
New York, NY 10021

The Archaeological Institute of America
Boston University
656 Beacon Street
Boston, MA 02215

Carnegie Museum of Art
440 Forbes Avenue
Pittsburgh, PA 15213

Cleveland Museum of Art
11150 East Boulevard
Cleveland, OH 44106

Elvehjem Museum of Art
University of Wisconsin
800 University Avenue
Madison, WI 53706

Indiana University Art Museum
Bloomington, IN 47405

J. Paul Getty Museum
17985 Pacific Coast Hwy
Malibu, CA 90265

Los Angeles County Museum of Art
5905 Wiltshire Boulevard
Los Angeles, CA 90036

The Metropolitan Museum of Art
1000 Fifth Avenue
New York, NY 10028

Museum of Fine Arts
465 Huntington Avenue
Boston, MA 02115

University of Virginia Alderman Library
Charlottesville, VA 22903

Washington University Libraries
Skinker and Lindell Boulevards
St. Louis, MO 63130

World Archaeological Society
120 Lakewood Drive
Hollister, MO 65672

CANADA

Ontario Archaeological Society
126 Willowdale Avenue
Willowdale
Ontario, M2N 4Y2

Royal Ontario Museum
100 Queens Park
Toronto
Ontario, M5S 2C6

UNITED KINGDOM

British Museum
Great Russell Street
London WC1B 3DG

Roman Palace and Museum
Fishbourne
Chichester PO19 3QR

Verulamium Museum
St. Albans AL3 4SW

ITALY

Capitoline Museums
Capitoline Hill, Rome

Museo Nazionale Romano
Viale delle Terme, Rome

**National
Archaeological Museum**
Via Museo, Naples

The Vatican Museum
The Vatican, Rome

Sites

UNITED KINGDOM
Arbeia Roman Fort
South Shields,
Tyne and Wear
Exhibits include personal
items of Roman soldiers.

Bignor Roman Villa
Bignor, West Sussex
Many fine mosaics.

Caerleon Roman Fortress
Caerleon, Gwent
Includes barracks, an
amphitheater, and baths.

Hadrian's Wall
Northumberland
Wall along the border of
Scotland and England.

Roman Baths
Stall Street, Bath
Well-preserved
Roman baths.

FRANCE
Arles, Provence
Remains of Roman city,
including amphitheater.

Nîmes, Provence
Remains include the
temple "Maison Carrée"
and an amphitheater.

Pont du Gard, near
Nîmes, Provence
Roman aqueduct.

GREECE
Athens
Remains of a Roman
arch, temple, odeon, and
other monuments.

ITALY
Hadrian's Villa
Tivoli, near Rome
Richest imperial villa in
the Roman empire.

Herculaneum and
Pompeii, near Naples
Well-preserved Roman
towns that were buried
when the volcano
Vesuvius erupted.

Oplontis
Well-preserved villa.

Ostia, Rome
Excavated ancient port of
the city of Rome

Rome
The famous colosseum
and many other well-
preserved remains.

LEBANON
Heliopolis,
northeast Lebanon
Ruins of a temple
precinct, including the
Temple of Jupiter-Ba'al.

SPAIN
Alcantara, on the Tagus
River, near the border of
Spain and Portugal
Roman arch bridge.

Italica
Oldest Roman town.
Birthplace of emperors
Trajan and Hadrian.

Segovia, north of Madrid
Famous aqueduct.

TUNISIA
Dougga, southwest
of Carthage
Ancient Roman city,
including an impressive
temple and theater.

TURKEY
Aphrodisias, south of Izmir
Best preserved temple in
Asia Minor

Ephesus, south of Izmir
Extensive archaeological
remains of Roman town
life. Also, ruins of Greek
Temple of Artemis.

Glossary

AEDILE
One of four government officers in charge of public buildings, markets, and games.

AMPHITHEATER
An oval-shaped theater in which gladiator contests were held.

AMPHORA
A narrow-necked, two-handled vessel used for transporting and storing olive oil, wine, or fish sauce.

AQUEDUCT
Underground or raised channel built to bring water into towns.

ATRIUM
A house's central hall, onto which most of the rooms of the house opened.

BARBARIAN
Term the Romans used to describe anyone who lived outside the empire.

BASILICA
A large public building, usually located in the forum, which was used mainly as law courts or for ceremonies.

BULLA
A good-luck charm worn by a boy.

CENSOR
A government official elected to keep a record of all Roman citizens, issue contracts for roads and temples, and revise Senate membership.

CENTURY
A company in the Roman army consisting of 80 men, led by an officer called a *centurion*.

CIRCUS
Stadium where chariot races were held.

CITIZEN
Status granted to free-born men (first, to those living in Italy; later, to all provincials; giving them privileges such as the right to vote.

COHORT
A unit in the Roman army – there were six centuries in a cohort.

CONSUL
One of a pair of elected politicians that shared the highest position in the Roman government.

CONTUBERNIUM
The smallest Roman army unit, consisting of eight soldiers.

DICTATOR
A state official who was granted complete control by the Senate in times of crisis.

DOMUS
A private family home.

EMPEROR
The supreme ruler of all Roman territories.

EMPIRE
The Empire was the period in Rome's history (c.31 B.C.–A.D. 476) when Rome was ruled by emperors. The empire (without a capital letter in this book) describes all of the territories ruled by Rome.

EQUESTRIAN
A wealthy social class descended from the first cavalry officers of the Roman army.

FORUM
Open area in a Roman town center, used as a marketplace and to air public business.

GLADIATOR
A specially trained fighter who battled other gladiators to the death in amphitheaters throughout the empire.

HYPOCAUST
Roman-designed central heating system in which hot air created by a fire flowed through cavities under floors and in walls.

INSULA
A large apartment building of mainly rented accommodation.

LARARIUM
A shrine, found in every Roman home, dedicated to the worship of the household gods.

LEGION
The main division in the Roman army, consisting of ten cohorts.

LUDI
Term used to describe Roman entertainment, such as sports events, games, or theater.

MOSAIC
A design or picture made with small pieces of stone, glass, or tile, usually cemented in a wall or floor.

ORATOR
A skilled public speaker.

PAPYRUS
An Egyptian water reed that was pressed out to make paper and then used for important Roman documents.

PLEBEIAN
A Roman citizen who was a member of the ordinary working class.

PRAETOR
A high-ranking, elected judge in the Roman state.

PRAETORIAN GUARD
An elite division of highly paid soldiers, founded by the emperor Augustus for protection.

PROCURATOR
Official in charge of looking after the finances in a province.

PROVINCIAL
A person who lived in one of the provinces governed by the Romans, but outside of Italy itself.

QUAESTOR
A government official elected to be responsible for the state's finances.

RELIEF
A carved or molded picture that stands out from its background.

REPUBLIC
Period in Rome's history (*c.*509-31 B.C.) when the empire was governed by a system of elected representatives.

SENATE
A group of politicians that met to decide on affairs of state such as military matters.

SLAVE
An individual without rights who was owned by another and used for various types of work.

STUCCO
Decorative plasterwork on walls and ceilings.

THERMAE
Roman public baths.

TOGA
Garment made from a (usually white) half-circle of cloth, which was draped around the body and worn by male citizens on formal occasions.

TRIBUNE
A government representative elected by the plebeians to protect their interests.

VILLA
A wealthy family's country house, often on a farming estate.

Index

Acknowledgments

Dorling Kindersley would like to thank:
Hilary Bird for the index. Elise Bradbury,
Connie Mersel, and Kristin Ward for
editorial assistance. Carlton Hibbert,
Myfanwy Hancock, and Kate Eagar for
design assistance. Caroline Potts and
Robert Graham for picture research
assistance. James Mills-Hicks for
cartography. Henry Gewanter for the
Roman coins. Paul Roberts (British
Museum) for help with historical data.

Photographs by:
Peter Anderson, Peter Chadwick, Mike
Dunning, Steven Gorton, Christi Graham,
Frank Greenaway, Peter Hayman, John
Hesteltine, Dave King, Liz McAulay, Andrew
McRobb, David Murray, Nick Nicholls,
Steven Oliver, Kim Sayer, Karl Shone, James
Stevenson, Clive Streeter, Matthew Ward.

Illustrations by:
David Ashby, Russell Barnett, Simone
Boni, Robin Carter, Steven Conlin,
John Davis, Peter Dennis, Paolo Donati,
Ray Grinaway, Kevin Jones Associates,
Thomas Keenes, Tony Morris,
Sarah Ponder, Sergio, John Temperton,
Peter Visscher, John Woodcock.

Picture credits: t = top b = bottom
c = center l = left r = right
The publisher would like to thank the
following for their kind permission to
reproduce the photographs:

Ancient Art and Architecture Collection
21cr, 55b; Ashmolean Museum of Art
and Archeology, Oxford, 16tl, 133c;
Bridgeman Art Library 132bl / Galleria
degli Uffizi, Florence 19b / Musee
Crozatier, Le Puys en Velais, France 23t /
Musee Granet, Aix-en-Provence 146cl;
The British Museum 23c, 31b, 56t, 57tr,
57c, 57bl, 65br, 94, 95tl, 95bl, 95bc, 101tr,
120bl, 120c, 120/121c, 121tc, 124, 125,
126/127; Capitoline Museum, Rome 19tr;
C.M. Dixon 129tr; E.T. Archive /
Archeological Museum, Naples 95br, /
Prenestino Museum, Rome 130 br; Mary
Evans Picture Library 46tr, 46c, 55t, 60c,
84c, 128cl; Werner Forman Archive 53bl;
Sonia Halliday 129bl; Simon James 1c,
21tl, 22/23, 30bl, 31tl, 36t, 39br, 40t, 40b,
45t, 51b, 66bl, 67bl, 74, 78b, 80r, 81b,
84bl, 93t, 96/97, 102c, 102/103b, 104,
105tl, 105b, 109t, 117bl, 123b, 131r,
jacket; The Mansell Collection 26r; Museo
Archeologico di Napoli 48tl, 48bl, 49cl,
49bl, 49r,130l; Museum of London 61t;
University Museum of Newcastle 76b, 77;
The Trustees of the National Museums of
Scotland 1995 2l, 5, 14tr, 39tr; The
Science Museum, London 3b, 58/59,
92/93, jacket; Tony Stone Images 12/13b;
Lin White 3cl, 14cl, 22bc, 32tl, 33b, 37tl,
37c, 41tr, 42/43, 44bl, 44cr, 47t, 47b, 52bl,
52br, 56br, 59t, 59c, 60b, 64t, 65bl, 87cl,
91cl, 92b, 98/99, 101tl, 103t, 108b, 110cl,
110b, 111, 112c, 113tr, 114/115, 117cl,
117cr, 119bl, 119br, 121br, 123cl, jacket;
Zefa Picture Library (UK) 87tl.

Every effort has been made to trace the copyright
holders and we apologise in advance for any
unintentional omissions. We would be pleased to
insert the appropriate acknowledgment in any
subsequent edition of this publication.